THE
SEXUAL
BOND

THE
SEXUAL
BOND

FRANÇOIS DUYCKAERTS

translated from the French by John A. Kay

Delacorte Press

Originally published in Belgium
by CHARLES DESSART ÉDITEUR
under the title *LA FORMATION DU LIEN SEXUEL*

Belgian edition copyright © 1964
by Charles Dessart, Bruxelles
Translation copyright © 1970
by Dell Publishing Co., Inc.

Library of Congress Catalog Card Number: 75-102804
Manufactured in the United States of America

First American Printing

DESIGNED BY *Barbara Kohn Isaac*

CONTENTS

PREFACE

Until recently, nobody thought that sexual behavior presented any problems. Once it had been explained as the outward manifestation of a single powerful drive directed toward the propagation of the species, it was thought that everything had been said that needed saying. But then came observation and analysis, and very soon the large number of factors involved and the complexity of their interaction made it necessary to abandon such an oversimplified explanation. Today we know that normal sexual behavior is simple only when it is seen in outline. Looked at more closely, and particularly in the light of pathological phenomena, it appears for what it is: a whole series of multiple reactions of great variety and complexity requiring a comparatively long period of time, and being by no means always successful.

From the first erotic excitement to the final possession of a partner, the road is long and rocky. Most of the stops along the way are now known to us, but we still have no satisfactory explanation of the path connecting them. The time has come to try to make a synthesis—similar to the one successfully undertaken in the past—with little data, and on the basis of a few ascetic and mystical experiences, by the authors of spiritual doctrine, who were concerned with tracing the road taken by the soul as it rose toward God. Such a comparison will probably shock both those who think that sex is undesirable and those who are blind to the part played by sublime love in ascetic and mystical experience. Nevertheless, it is both legitimate and a source of valuable information in considering the nature of human beings as a whole. The works of the mystics are incomprehensible to those who are ignorant of the language of sex and love. Similarly, to write a description of the stages by which a man and a woman, starting poles apart, come together and achieve mutual possession is no frivolous nor obscene task. Indeed, it goes far beyond mere psychological interest: the sex life of human beings provides a basic image, a sort of fundamental prototype reflecting the major social, moral and religious attitudes of the human race. Viewing things from this angle, I believe that a detailed analysis of the stages which mark the road to a happy sex life will help not only those who may have difficulties in this respect, but also the very large number of people who wish to gain a better understanding of broader human problems, such as those of violence and reason, war and peace, sin and grace.

For the starting point of my analysis I have chosen not childhood but adult life. In most works on sex, the author starts at birth, runs through the major phases of growth (infancy, school days, puberty, adolescence, youth and maturity) and shows how each of them contributes to a complete and harmonious sex life, which is considered the culmina-

tion of an evolutionary process. This is a strictly chronological approach whose landmarks are age and activity—
entry into a school or profession, marriage—in other words,
social factors correlated with biological and psychological
data. This is the approach that has given us the well-known
distinctions among sex life in infancy, puberty and maturity and, within infancy, among oral, anal, phallic and
genital stages. In the coming pages, I have tried to avoid
this method, however useful and legitimate it may be, because in my view it tends too often to confuse natural and
civil data, and biological, psychological and social considerations. I have done my best to remain strictly in the psychological field.

It is for this reason that, while I have not neglected the
information provided by developmental psychology, I have
started with a biologically mature man or woman with a
complete genital system (organs, nervous system and endo-
crine glands).

Daily experience shows that even for adults, the path
from erotic stimulation to the consummation of a heterosexual act is marked by a striking series of psychological
events which follow one another at varying intervals of
time, from a few minutes to several years. This same series
of intervening psychological events occurs even in the most
favorable circumstances of happily married life, although
they may follow each other very rapidly, as in electronic
devices where light flashes from one point to another as
fast as the eye can follow. At other times, as with young
people not yet joined in matrimony, the psychological
journey takes much longer, sometimes months or years. In
the most unhappy cases, the pause at one of the way sta-
tions along the journey is so long that it becomes a complete block, and the goal is never reached. In this book I
shall pay only incidental attention to the length of time
taken by the journey; I shall rather concentrate on each of

the stages leading from the initial sexual emotion to the consummation of the sex act.

But what is a complete sex act? It seems to me that we must accept as a fact that there are pairs of human beings for whom the consummation of the sex act provides a release which is perfect in itself, and which abolishes, in a moment of great pleasure, the separation of body and soul. This is surely an objective fact, even though it can be understood only through personal experience. It is a fact in the same way as a great work of literature is a fact, even though it may be inaccessible to animals or Philistines. It would not be nonscientific to analyze the inspirations, dreams, angers, hopes and disappointments of the author, and his drafts and proofs, corrected and recorrected, before the appearance of a complete and perfect work. Similarly, it is not merely subjective to assume as a starting point that two beings of different sexes can achieve an orgasm that is special to them, without which the whole process is only perversion, preparation or caricature.

This book is, apparently, intended to have wide appeal, and when I was asked to write it, I was told it should be a "popularization." I prefer not to use that word. It implies something faintly dishonorable to me: explaining the conquests of science to ignorant people in oversimplified, "popular" terms. It seems to me that science is like a hard-working laborer who, by the sweat of his brow, brings to the surface of knowledge a mass of material which he has little time to polish, and still less to present to the public in an attractive package worthy of the contents. One of the great merits of scientists is that they *are* hard working; it is therefore only right to take their discoveries seriously and, whenever possible, to explain them. I shall therefore try to explain in ordinary language what many years of laborious research has taught modern psychologists about the complexities of sexual behavior. This does not seem to me to be rewriting psychology in "popular" terms; rather, I shall try to give it that place of distinction which is its due, and to show its human side, which is often not understood.

Although the best parts of this book must be attributed to the pioneers of sexual psychology—Havelock Ellis, Freud, Jung, Stekel, Schwarz, Hesnard, Lagache and many others—I have tried as far as possible to avoid burdening the text with footnotes. The ideas of these authors· are so well known that there is no need to refer to them on each separate occasion. Moreover, the debt we owe these bold explorers can hardly be paid by quoting sections of their work out of context in footnotes. The reader will observe that every line of this book is influenced and inspired by their discoveries, and if there is any value in my synthesis, it will be entirely due to these illustrious forerunners. I have borrowed not merely one or two ideas from them, but the whole spirit of their work.

In conclusion, I must thank two of my colleagues at the University of Liège, Mr. Albert Husquinet and Mr. Marc Richelle, for helping me remove some inaccuracies, and even errors, from my text. I can only hope that all my readers will show the same spirit of goodwill and constructive criticism.

F.D.

THE
SEXUAL
BOND

I

STIMULATION
AND INHIBITION

Before beginning this study, I want to make one point quite clear: in discussing sexual emotions and behavior, I have confined myself to explanations that relate to the workings of the mind. This is not because I am unaware of the great importance of the state of the reproductive organs, the balance or lack of balance of the hormonal secretions and the delicate adjustment of the nervous and glandular systems. But in the field of sexual behavior, more than in any other, we must take care not to confuse different points of view. In no other field of science is there such a great danger of introducing hidden attitudes, prejudices and dreams, and confusing them with objective knowledge. Because we have to find solutions to problems of sexual behavior every day, we find it difficult not to take sides when making an objective study of them. Thus, a physiologist will often introduce psychological or moral considerations into his work when these are, often without his knowing it, no more than reflections of his personal attitude toward sex. In the same way, when a psychologist stumbles upon mysteries that his current work is unable to clarify, he is often tempted to fall back upon oversimplified physiological explanations in the hope of filling in the gaps in his psychological knowledge, and thus escaping from a state of uncertainty that is most disturbing when dealing with this delicate subject.

We should venture only cautiously into realms of which we have little knowledge; it is safer to trust the specialists, and not to claim universal knowledge. In writing this book, I have sworn not to make excursions into the related sciences, especially sexual physiology, but to confine myself strictly to a psychological study. This does not mean that I look down upon explanations derived from knowledge of the human organism, but rather that I know my own limitations and wish to be precise.

But before we can leave aside all discussion of organic factors in human sexual behavior, I must state my starting point: I shall be dealing only with adult human beings with sexual organs in good physiological condition. Otherwise, it would be difficult to distinguish physiology from psychology. In considering the embryonic sex life of a prepubertal child, for example, how is it possible to ignore the fact that the organs and nervous and glandular systems are immature? A whole range of psychological factors, such as incomplete understanding of the differences between male and female bodies, are very closely bound up with the fact that the organs are not yet mature; this fact alone deprives children of the concrete experience they need in order to understand the sexual parts of their bodies. We know that the time lag between sexual and intellectual development, which is special to human beings, is of the greatest significance, but as long as this time lag exists it is difficult, if not impossible, to determine all the psychological aspects of sexual relationships: all will not become apparent until sexual contact becomes physiologically possible. While it is no doubt true that many of the psychological features of adult sex life can be explained by this time lag in the pre-pubertal period, it is nevertheless true that before study-ing the origins of sex life, we must know it in its adult form. For, once a sex life becomes physiologically possible, the psychological processes connected with the establish-ment of sexual relations will appear without more ado; to describe them will be to describe all the mental and emo-tional transformations that take place between the first genuine erotic excitement and a satisfactory heterosexual orgasm.

In connection with sex life, what is the meaning of the phrase "a human being with adult organs"? I mean by this any man or woman whose organs, glands and sexual system are ready to operate in a normal manner, and whose age is somewhere between fourteen and twenty—earlier for women, later for men—in the lower range and, at the upper, the rather vague period coinciding with the meno-pause for women and the beginning of old age for men. As we have little information about the sex life of older people, it would be unwise to select any precise age for the start of the decline of sexual powers. Even an event as char-acteristic as the menopause does not necessarily mean a weakening of erotic potential. It does seem likely that when ovulation ceases and the individual's general abili-ties decline, the whole sexual system undergoes major changes and loses its efficiency, but even this conclusion is thrown in doubt by the intense love life of certain elderly people, famous examples of whom are Jules Michelet and Victor Hugo. We would have to know far better than we do the real laws governing the decline of the human or-ganism before we could venture to explain these late-burning fires, whose brilliance is sometimes greater than those of youth or maturity. We might perhaps find that in old age a person benefits from earlier momentum, and makes up for declining physical strength by the force of his imagination and the intensity of his thoughts, which are less rapidly affected by age than his body. However this may be, the period following the climacteric crisis is just as special as the one before maturity, which we call puberty. The psychological nature of sexual relations during these periods of formation or decline are sufficiently special to deserve a separate study, which can indeed hardly be carried out successfully without a prior knowledge of normal adult sexual psychology. It is for these reasons that my present study is restricted to human beings at the peak of biological maturity.

This peak is attained at about age eighteen for girls and twenty for boys. Puberty is over, and boys and girls alike have a complete sexual system. The testicles and ovaries give off spermatozoa and eggs, respectively. The internal channels (oviducts and canals) and the copulatory organs (penis and vagina) are ready to bring the reproductory products of the male and female bodies together for fertilization. Furthermore, the science of endocrinology has recently revealed the major role played in the formation and function of the sexual apparatus by the circulating products called hormones, which at this stage are fully developed, while the nervous and the cerebrospinal systems are both ready to carry the sexual reflexes, first those that stimulate the fibers connected with emotions and then those that arm the genital muscles, without which erection and coitus cannot take place.

A detailed description of the sexual system is not necessary here; many may be found in works on physiology. But when this system comes to maturity, there is one result which is of direct interest to the psychologist: the individual then reaches the threshold of his or her normal erotic excitability. Before puberty and the achievement of biological maturity, the organism is sensitive to external erotic stimuli only occasionally and then at a rather low level of response. With the development of the sexual apparatus this sensitivity rapidly increases, reaching its normal level at the age of about twenty. At this time, and by means which are not yet fully understood, all sorts of things which, although they were perceived, had little or no effect on the organism, change their neutral character and become erotic stimuli. Certain colors, qualities of touch, forms, odors and sounds emanating from fellow humans detach themselves from the neutral background of the outside world and trigger sexual behavior in an organism that is now sensitive to them. The possession of this sensitivity to natural erotic stimuli is the point of departure of my study, and I am assuming that it has reached its normal level. I am well aware that this hypothesis represents a simplification of the facts, but it has the advantage of placing the fundamental problem of human sex life in proper perspective.

One question arises immediately: How and why does it come about that erotic stimuli acting on a sensitive organism do not immediately set in motion the whole train of sexual behavior? This question also applies to a number of subhuman species in which sexual contact is also invariably preceded by a longer or shorter period of preparation (known as pair-formation), but it is particularly relevant in connection with the human race, where, between the first erotic stimulations and the consummation of the sex act the interval is longer and is filled with more events and kinds of emotions than in any other species.

1

This lengthy interval between the awakening of a need and its satisfaction is special to sex. With other physiological needs, only a few hours at the most separate the onset of the first sensations of discomfort from acts likely to put matters right. Examples are hunger and the elimination of human waste. In the case of sex, however, many erotic stimuli may periodically affect the organism without leading to any deliberate and conscious completion of the sex act, except perhaps after a long period, running into months or years. How is this difference to be explained? I would like to start by pointing out that the sex instinct is different from the other fundamental instincts by its very nature. If it is to be fulfilled normally, the agreement of another human being of the opposite sex is essential. The target of the sexual drive is thus a living being and, in the case of the human race, a person—one whose grounds for refusal and whose opportunities for flight have been considerably enlarged by the development of language, memory and thought. Before we eat an apple, we do not ask it whether it agrees to this fate. The objects of such appetite are inanimate; if they are animate, we kill them by force, using our superior abilities. In the realm of sex, however, this use of force is called rape, and it always represents an unsatisfactory means of fulfilling a need. It is the very essence of the sex instinct that it requires a minimum of agreement by the mate, at least at the moment of copulation.

This special nature of the target of the sex instinct may put us on the road toward an objective explanation of the time lapse between stimulation and complete satisfaction. It is only very rarely that a person who feels erotically stimulated by the body of a possible mate will find immediate consent. Whether rightly or wrongly, he begins by believing that the person in question will refuse or at least hesitate.

On the one hand, in most studies of sex the impression is given that it is never the male who hesitates and that he is always ready to accept advances from any female whatsoever; on the other hand, it is said, the female hesitates and, in every known species, starts by adopting a defensive attitude to male advances, accepting them only later. The study of animal behavior almost daily reveals new exceptions to this oversimplification, which may have been formulated on the basis of the cultural models within which the observer himself lived. The fact is that there are many animal species in which sexual advances are made by the females, and the males start by resisting. Moreover, even in species where the initiative is usually taken by the male, there are many couples who reverse the normal behavior. In the human race, in any event, the initiative is sometimes taken by the man, sometimes by the woman. As soon as any group of human beings becomes even slightly homogeneous, it develops cultural models which favor initiative-taking by men or by women, and often a balance between the two. Why this should be still remains to be discovered by anthropologists. In many social groups a distinction is made in practice, if not in theory, between the *concealed* initiative which is expected from the women, who are required only to adopt seductive attitudes, and the *open* initiative adopted by the men, consisting, for example, in making the first advances and declaring their feelings. Even among the most virile men in our society there are many who wait for the woman to take the initiative in word or in attitude before making an open declaration.

The truth is that when a man and a woman find themselves together, they are filled with hesitation arising from the special nature of the instinct involved. As consent is required, the question is, Who will take the first step? This is a difficult problem, the solution to which is provided by tradition and even perhaps by heredity, and the form it takes is very much ritualized, as if the purpose were to avoid the need for individuals to find a satisfactory solution for themselves on each separate occasion.

But regardless of the attributes peculiar to men or women in taking the sexual initiative, there is always one partner who appears to attack and the other who starts by resisting. Consent is never immediate, unless the partners are living in full moral and sexual harmony. And even then the worries of daily life and irritating minor conflicts, and such things as differences in the physiological states, mean that a certain amount of time is usually needed to reach agreement, even though this time is, admittedly, often fairly short. Moreover, even with an ideal couple, agreement has to be found anew on each individual occasion. And in this repeated process the various stages which marked the original event will be found in compressed or very shortened form. Every time the partners come together in sexual union the various phases through which they passed in their original mating will be repeated in condensed and rapid form, much as ontogenesis reproduces in brief the long-term search of phylogenesis.

Since any man or woman who allows sexual excitement to develop unhindered is bound to be irresistibly drawn toward the partner while still risking the chance of a refusal, he or she remains on the defensive, setting up at least a temporary inhibition against triggering the cycle of sexual behavior. The need to obtain at least preliminary consent requires holding spontaneous reactions in suspense. Being uncertain of the attitude of the potential partner, the admirer is chary of allowing himself to be carried away by erotic emotions. Consequently, whether it is the man or the woman who is on the defensive, the result is always the same: there is a period of wariness, a suspension of emotion, and a refusal to allow the development of internal excitement.

It is this refusal to be carried away by early stimulation that we call inhibition. It will be stronger or weaker depending upon the partner's characteristics and upon the fears or moral principles of the person stimulated. But there is every evidence that it always occurs at the beginning of any erotic excitement whatsoever, regardless of the status of the partners—whether relatives, strangers or even spouses. I shall discuss each of these three cases in detail.

2

If the stimulation comes from a close relative (father, brother, mother, sister, adolescent child), social taboos provide a powerful brake. In this situation, not only do the individuals emitting the stimuli possess their own power of refusal, which may vary with their inclination or mood, in addition, they are supported by a collective refusal. We are all in fact in permanent contact with a large number of people who give off erotic signals, often without our noticing them, and whom we would expect on principle to reject any advances we might make. They will resist not only because in any new relationship any advance is bound to be met by some defensive action, but also because their resistance is that of society as a whole. They are expressing a general taboo that goes far beyond their personal disposition.

Human societies have always regulated sexual contacts. In all places and at all times civil or religious authority has intervened to distinguish what is permitted from what is not. In one group no contact is allowed before marriage; in another it may be permitted both before and outside marriage, but even in such a group it is rarely encouraged, and there are always restrictions based on age and degree of kinship. The science of cultural anthropology describes the many rules that societies establish to regulate the sexual behavior of their members in the way best suited to them.

Of all taboos, the most nearly universal is the taboo on incest. It is the common denominator and probably the origin of all customary and legal controls of sexual activity —given, of course, that the term "incest" is taken in a broad sense, rather than in the narrow one of sexual intercourse between father and daughter or mother and son. The prohibition on incest is really a summary of all the rules governing marriage. It means that a man may not take any woman he chooses without restriction. Within certain specific degrees of kinship, which vary from culture to culture and society to society, individuals are forbidden to live together permanently for the purpose of procreation.

Among contemporary anthropologists, Claude Lévi-Strauss has certainly produced the most enlightening study of the many forms of the ban on incest and of its basic meaning. In a flash of insight, he sees it as the meeting place between the realm of nature, or the sphere of natural instincts, and the realm of culture, which governs the satisfaction of these instincts by rules and laws. He feels that the incest taboo has a positive meaning as one of the basic modes of communication between human groups.[1] He writes, indeed, that "the incest taboo is less a rule preventing a man from marrying his mother, sister or daughter, than a rule compelling him to *give* his mother, sister or daughter to someone else."[2] Without some rule of this kind —that is, without an obligation to give the women of one's

[1] Claude Lévi-Strauss, *Les Structures élémentaires de la parenté*, Paris, P.U.F., 1949, p. 613.
[2] *Ibid.*, p. 596.

clan to the men of another, or without this organized exchange of women—human groupings would soon have exploded or would have continued splitting up into hostile or mutually estranged families, shut in upon themselves and with no doors or windows on the world. And no preordained harmony could have prevented the proliferation and mutual antagonism of these groups.[3] Behind all the marriage rules, Lévi-Strauss always finds a system of exchange. In short, he feels, in a striking phrase, that the ban on incest "c'est la règle du don par excellence."[4]

To a sex psychologist, the most interesting part of Lévi-Strauss's theory is its implications. For, if it was necessary to create an obligatory system of exchange to regulate the possession of women, and particularly the women closest to the man concerned, this must have been because they were the objects of his strongest desire. The strength of an interdiction is proportional to the strength of the desire.

In some civilizations only gods and royalty may overstep the ban and marry a father, brother, sister, son or daughter. In these very exemptions is the key to the meaning of the ban. Those who bear the heavy burden of supreme responsibility are granted complete freedom. He who makes the law cannot be bound by the law. He has the right to yield to his deepest and most natural instincts. Is this not an acknowledgment that the earliest and most powerful sex stimuli are those that are closest, among members of the family or clan?

Let us ignore for the time being the persons in the family between whom sexual relations are permitted—husband and wife—and take a look at what happens with the others: father, mother, adolescent children, adult brothers and sisters.

[3] *Ibid.*, p. 593.
[4] *Ibid.*, p. 596.

Within the family, the opposite sexes live close together in surroundings that are particularly favorable to the awakening of erotic impulses. Individuals of both sexes offer each other, usually without knowing it, all the stimuli of color, movement, odor and form that are likely to set in motion the whole cycle of sexual behavior. I mention only the most obvious examples: the boy intrigued by the anatomy of his sister or mother, the girl by that of her brother or father. The mere fact that they live in the same place may bring a detail fraught with erotic significance to the surface of an adolescent's mind; that detail in itself may start the whole chain of sexual reactions.

By entering into people's thoughts and dreams, psychoanalysts often uncover incestuous desires. This may even be the most significant contribution psychoanalysts have made to the psychology of human relations. Despite, or perhaps because of, the strict ban on incest, society cannot prevent those nearest to us from providing our first erotic stimuli. While it is true that in most cases these early stimuli do not in fact set off the whole cycle of sexual behavior, there are still a number of subtle factors that are likely to do so, and society has found it necessary to counteract them by inventing a complicated system of internal prohibitions.

It has been claimed that the psychoanalysts' findings about incestuous desires are valid only in our bourgeois Western society. I do not believe this is true. We have only to consider the rigid rules governing sexual unions in all human societies, however primitive, to be forced to agree that the human race has always and everywhere been compelled to struggle against the centripetal and incestuous forces of the family unit. But it is true that our society, by limiting the individual's freedom to act outside the family unit, has at the same time increased the sexual significance of members of the family itself.

Furthermore, if we understand how strong the links are

between the external erotic stimuli and the mechanisms that set off sexual behavior—recent work in animal psychology has explained this cause and effect very well—we should be convinced that any single member of the family circle may have dangerous sexual significance for any other member. The extent of the significance varies from situation to situation, depending upon three determining factors: first, the type of aura radiated by the person who possesses the sexual qualities; second, the degree to which that person makes use of these qualities; and, third, the sexual sensitivity of the stimulated person whose threshold of excitation will be progressively lower as fewer opportunities are presented for the release of his urges. Let us deal for the moment only with the last of these factors.

If life outside the family circle provides unmarried persons with no opportunity for satisfying their sexual instincts, we must expect to find them reacting to the slightest stimuli, no matter what the source. The result is that the sexually best endowed members of the family become more and more attractive.

It is only because these sexual reactions are blocked at their very onset that in the ordinary course of life, and unless they have gone for psychotherapy, human beings deny that they have incestuous desires. Their denials are sincere. Never, or almost never, has the unconscious permitted the sexual mechanism to be triggered by stimulation from a close relative. It is only when the voluntary controls are relaxed, as in dreams or on the analyst's couch, that incestuous stimuli come to the surface. On waking up, or on returning to daily life, the controls operate again and the release mechanism is blocked. The consequence is that, despite the many erotic stimulations to which they have been exposed, a large number of biologically mature individuals have never felt sexual or erotic excitement in the presence of even the most attractive members of their families. But the fact that the individual is unaware does not mean that a special relationship has not been established between an erotic feature of some member of the family and his sexual urge.

Then what causes the block? Psychology has a long way to go before it can answer this question. For it can hardly be claimed that the ban on incest or the many social or moral taboos described by anthropologists and sociologists are sufficient. Psychologists know that taboos are frequently ineffective and fail to deter many individuals. And this leads us to question: How do these moral taboos act in practice? How do they manage to exert their influence? We know only too well that the actual words of a prohibition do not carry enough weight to exert any ultimate influence. My own personal view is that these moral taboos have an effect only when they are transmitted by the parents. Parents express both social and moral taboos by their reserved attitudes, even down to such details as rejecting a kiss, raising the voice, showing bad temper, refusing to be seen in the nude, locking the bedroom door, or avoiding unnecessary physical contact. And the taboo concealed in these ritualistic details is well understood by the beholder. The individual senses the ban on incest long before he understands it. It is first communicated to him by parental attitudes; only later does he become consciously aware of it.

Students of animal behavior have shown that in the subhuman world, certain kinds of ritualized conduct act as triggers, setting off reactions in the desired mate. Precopulatory dances are examples of behavior patterns that have lost their functional value and have instead become stimulatory signals. On the other side of the picture, we should ask whether any ritual forms of conduct inhibit erotic excitement. We can surely agree that some do, even if we consider only the forms of behavior connected with modesty. Involving as they do the concealment and pretended nonexistence of the sexual parts of the body, they are without doubt symbolic expressions of refusal. Usually, without even being aware of it, close relatives give off numerous inhibitory signals at the slightest sign of sexual danger.

If we analyze these inhibitory signals, we shall see that aggressive factors predominate. A father who is too attracted to his daughter's youthful beauty will not hesitate to become distant, scornful and hostile, unless he is capable of recognizing his own sexual impulse without danger; most often he overcomes the attraction he feels for this woman of his own blood by acting exactly opposite to his feelings. The tragedy is that if excessive severity arises from an excess of desire, it may end by becoming an erotic signal in itself.

However that may be, the ambiguousness of the family situation is obvious. On the one hand, daily proximity and the erotic auras that close relatives, like all other human beings, carry with them, make them the nearest sources of sexual stimulation. On the other hand, these relatives put out so many inhibiting signals that an almost instantaneous block is created in the system that sets off the sexual cycle. And it is this self-contradictory situation that causes so much trouble during the "difficult age."

The most logical way of escaping from the frustrating conflict would be to permit exposure to erotic stimuli outside the family. Unfortunately, this course, too, presents difficulties. Even outside the family, the mere fact that the cycle of sexual behavior has been triggered does not mean that intercourse will take place easily and freely. For even outside the family, the sexual process is far from being set in motion spontaneously.

3

When men and women find themselves together, they do
not immediately start the natural sexual cycle. Even the
most libertine or the boldest go through a preparatory
phase, the length and course of which depend both on the
resistance of the one being wooed and on the experience
of the wooer. The most discreet restrict themselves to a
chaste courtship and engage in intercourse only after marriage. But with any couple there are what may be called
preliminaries. Even the lowest kind of prostitution, where
intercourse is almost instantaneous and automatic, and
where there appears to be no psychological preparation, is
no exception to the general rule. In the first place, there
is a series of conventions to be respected, even if these only
take the form of a proffer of money or material goods.
Moreover, a person visiting a prostitute for the first time
does so only after long deliberations, which may have
lasted days, months, or even years. The prostitute herself
has probably engaged in this form of sexual behavior only
after a series of disturbing experiences, involving frustra-
tions and faltering efforts to find satisfaction in many other
directions. In any event, even among the most primitive
peoples, prostitution exists only on the fringes of society.
And it would be a complete misunderstanding of the facts
to consider prostitution, which is a phenomenon typical of
an advanced civilization—at least in the complex and systematic form in which we know it today—as an example
of natural behavior, held in check only by social conventions. Prostitution is really much more a device adopted to
overcome the difficulty of ensuring that everyone, both
male and female, enjoys a normal sex life. It should on no
account be considered as a model for natural sex relations.

We must therefore be careful to distinguish between the

preparatory phase of sexual behavior and the act itself. Between the moment of the first erotic stimulation and the consummation of intercourse a fairly long time intervenes, occupied both in overcoming the partner's resistance and in breaking down the barriers within the wooer himself. Furthermore, both of these are but different aspects of a single phenomenon: the mental opposition that the earliest sexual desires always arouse in every single human being, even when these desires are directed toward individuals who are not tabooed by law or custom. However strange it may seem, the block still develops, just as when desire occurs between two close relatives.

A simplified view of primitive man, one that has arisen more as a reflection of our own desires than as a result of knowledge of the actual facts, has led us to believe that in most tribes relations between young men and young women take place freely, whenever they feel the desire and a favorable opportunity occurs. Nothing is further from the truth. Even the least oppressive societies require both young people to go through a whole series of formal observances; only when they have scrupulously carried out these observances under the supervision of their elders are they permitted to consummate the sex act. The observances are initiation rites, and their very existence is evidence that human beings do not permit their young to surrender themselves to the pleasures of sexual intercourse whenever they wish. In the gentle Arapesh tribe, the elders do not hesitate to frighten youngsters approaching puberty, who may be tempted by the idea of sexual relations, by describing in detail the horrible effects on health and physical beauty of premature intercourse. The young Arapesh girl knows that if she has sexual experiences before puberty or before her puberty is officially recognized, "her breasts will continue to stand up, small and stiff and inhospitable, instead of falling in the luxuriant heaviness that the Arapesh consider to be the high point of female beauty."[5]

While there may be great variety in the customs regulating the sexual behavior of young people, all of them have one thing in common: they make life very difficult for the young man who wants to approach a young woman for the purpose of possessing her sexually. Everywhere, there is a prescribed path, which is considered the normal route. Along the way are certain stopping places—rituals, preordained pauses and time lapses—and the whole process has a fixed overall duration. Naturally there are shortcuts and secret ways; these are strongly disapproved of by the adults, but the more impatient youths follow them nevertheless, taking the usual precautions. Whichever route an individual chooses, there are always obstacles to be overcome, trials to be borne, more or less disagreeable preliminary feats to be accomplished.

The usual psychoanalytical explanations have led us to believe that the blocking of the sex instinct at puberty is mainly due to the moral and social bans that adult society imposes. Although these explanations are certainly not to be rejected, they present only one aspect of the problem, and one type of cause. For, what is the true origin of these bans and taboos? If we look at the matter from the biological angle we might be tempted to reverse cause and effect, and to say that the moral bans are not mere prohibitions: they embrace a whole set of positive rites whose purpose is to remove the initial block that arises when men and women meet for the first time, and to endow instinctive actions with greater value and greater human significance.

In truth, the two explanations should be accepted side by side. First, it is clearly a psychological necessity to have

[5] Margaret Mead, *Sex and Temperament in Three Primitive Societies*, New York, Dell Publishing Co., Inc., 1968, p. 98.

a certain number of rites and behavior patterns that must be gone through to overcome instinctive inhibitions and achieve sexual intercourse under the conditions imposed by human nature and society. Second, no doubt for reasons connected with prestige and wealth, in no society have the adults failed to take advantage of their superiority to increase the number, difficulty and duration of the tests that must be gone through before the sex act may be performed.

While every society has over a period of time devised methods of its own for releasing inhibitions and humanizing the procedures by which young people approach one another, its adults and leaders have never failed to make the process more burdensome and to turn it to their own benefit. Viewed in this light, the conflict between socially acceptable and forbidden behavior is merely the struggle between traditional methods—fixed by custom and law and approved by the influential adults in the social group —and more personal, less common methods, which because of the pressures of tradition have to be practiced in secret. We should not be too ready to believe that on the outer fringes of society everything is straightforward and uninhibited, and that there is no slow and tortuous preparation for acts of pleasure.

In answer to those who argue that inhibitions affect only the young people of a particular social group or operate only in connection with special decisions governed by the rules of social behavior, marriage and its preliminaries for example, I would point out that even among experienced adults who are unrestrained by any explicit taboos, it takes quite a long time for couples to come together. It is often only as the result of special circumstances (a party, a ceremony, war, isolation in a private place, excitement or stimulation by liquor) that potential partners find the courage to make the first advances. And a whole set of such special circumstances, both external and internal, is needed before they will declare themselves. This does not mean that erotic excitement occurs only on these occasions, but rather that in the ordinary circumstances of daily life a brake is put on it as soon as it appears.

What happens to a person who is ready to respond to external sex stimuli when a possible mate enters his field of perception? The sex mechanism is not immediately stimulated or set in motion. For the forms, colors and odors of another person's body to have a stimulating effect, it is essential that the man or woman in question should not appear as a potential enemy. He or she must be seen straight off as benevolent, someone whose hypnotic influence can be risked without fear of harm or loss of independence. We all know that when our sexual emotions are aroused, our consciences are lulled and our defenses undermined, and so we are prepared to risk being fascinated by sexual stimuli only when they emanate from someone we know to be well disposed toward us. As soon as even the slightest aggressive intention appears, our defensive system is alerted, our conscience is awakened, and the entire nervous and hormonal systems stand ready to reinforce our muscles for flight or attack. Because sexuality has been deprived of the use of the forces now assembled for defense, its sensitivity to erotic stimuli diminishes, thus neutralizing any powers of seduction the other person may possess.

It is an oversimplification to consider that once an individual has become sensitive to erotic stimuli, all members of the opposite sex automatically appear to be well disposed. Even a mate allowed by law or custom arouses suspicion when he or she first appears on the scene; except for long-standing friends or acquaintances, everyone is a potential enemy before becoming a possible mate. Even though the danger may be purely imaginary, it is only prudent to act cautiously and to be prepared to deal with friend or foe as the case may be.

Recent work in animal psychology has brought to light a phenomenon of considerable significance in the human world as well. It has been found that most animals do not merely live in groups, but carve out territories for themselves and act as if the defense of their territory were more important than mating. Desmond Morris, for example, has shown that male sticklebacks cannot help treating the females entering their territory as enemies before accepting them as mates. Their first reaction is to combat the invasion of their territory; only later do they respond sexually.[6] This observation also throws light on human behavior.

A human being has far more than a territory to defend: he has a family that keeps him alive, even if it is sometimes less generous than he would wish; he has an inheritance which he already enjoys or will shortly enjoy; he has habits to which he clings because they give him all the pleasures to which he is accustomed without too much inconvenience; he has a circle of friends with unspoken but nonetheless hard-and-fast conventions, and a whole mental and emotional system to protect him from internal disturbances that might be too violent or too anarchical. And now a stranger enters his carefully protected territory. His first reaction will be a suspicious look, filled with a mixture of fear and hope. The question is inevitable: "Will I have to defend myself against insidious attack, or can I hope for unexpected pleasures?" At the very moment his sexual emotions are aroused, he is confronted with a possible threat to the moral and physical integrity of his very existence.

[6] Desmond Morris, "The Function and Causation of Courtship Ceremonies," in *L'Instincte dans le comportement des animaux et de l'homme*, Paris, Masson, 1956, p. 278.

This notion of personal territory throws light on one of the greatest paradoxes of the psychology of sex: How is it that pleasant stimuli or stimuli announcing future pleasures can so rapidly become disagreeable, even unbearable? One answer could be that while the stimuli are agreeable, they are also felt to be a threat, an attack against the territory which is an extension of the personality. In Freudian language, the person with an erotic aura is at first felt to be a possible castrator, and the sexual stimuli emanating from him or her are bound to seem inimical. The fear is that the stimuli are a means to gain entrance to the citadel; afterward, the invader may wish to lay down the law.

These notions of *territory* and *intrusion* are both new and vitally important. In their natural state, animals come together in colonies and stake out one or more exclusive areas. The same thing occurs among human beings when they form youth clubs, social clubs, recreation clubs or fraternities. These groups are not necessarily shut in on themselves, but they all possess a domain or territory, whether it is a neighborhood, a bar or a district. Although they may be similar to one another in form or structure, they each have their distinct and separate area of operation, and any outsider who ventures into this area will be received with suspicion or even downright hostility.

To return to the problem of sex relations, let us see what happens to a mixed group of friends when a female outsider enters the area. She upsets everything. Over a period of months, or perhaps years, these people have become adjusted to one another's ways. They have discovered just what distance must be maintained between individuals to prevent the disintegration of the group. Since the group's collective instinct for self-preservation has been as strong as that of any individual, none of its members has been permitted to fall under the overwhelming influence of an outsider. So if an outsider—a very attractive girl—makes advances to a male member of the group, it is not difficult to predict the consequences. The group as a whole may absorb the newcomer while preventing her from seducing an individual member; it may reject any member who permits himself to be seduced by the unassimilable outsider; and the contest among the males may be so fierce that the group disintegrates. Of these three possibilities, the first is the least likely, since the outsider will probably frighten every member of the group—the girls because she may well dethrone them, the boys because they fear an internecine struggle, and the young man most involved because he fears rejection by the group and loss of the emotional satisfactions with which membership had provided him.

Both during adolescence and later, human beings cast a suspicious eye on anyone who trespasses on their territory. Outsiders have a special fascination because their erotic appeal has not been staled by familiarity. And it is precisely this fascination that makes the person whose territory is invaded so mistrustful. Does it not foreshadow wholesale expropriation, and surrender to the intruder, of all the physical and moral benefits the occupant previously enjoyed?

If a person's Ego is defined as the total organization of his desires and his emotional investment in the outside world, it is reasonable to assume that any potential mate, as soon as he or she emits erotic signals, whether deliberately or not, is likely to appear a threat to the Ego. And the more intense the signals become, the more they will disturb and threaten the psychological equilibrium achieved after years of careful adaptation to circumstances.

In consequence, erotic stimulation has an aggressive component in its early stages; it is this that explains the attitude of watchful caution on the part of the person stimulated. Young people without sexual experience and adults looking for new adventures are alike in attributing a certain amount of hostility to those who send erotic signals in their direction. If it is a man who is making the advance, the woman shies off and thinks that aggressiveness is a male attribute. If it is a woman who makes the first advances, the man becomes increasingly wary and tends to feel that aggressiveness is a feminine characteristic.

Psychology has traditionally tended to oversimplify matters, and—as I mentioned before—to set as a rule that men are sexually active and aggressive while women are passive and easily frightened. (This may be because psychologists focussed their attention exclusively on their own cultures, and also because of personal factors: for many years psychology was practiced almost exclusively by men; their scientific objectivity may have been insufficient to overcome a nostalgic attachment to the idea of virility.) Today we know that there are societies in which the roles are reversed: the women take the initiative and the men wait to be chosen—as do the Tchambuli of the South Seas, for example.[7] In our own society, too, we often come across provocative women and passive men; there are even whole groups where this arrangement is quite normal. But in any case the sex that is allowed to take the initiative always seems by that fact to be the more aggressive. So true is this that, particularly when sex signals are emitted deliberately and persistently, they always seem to contain some element of aggression, and so produce in the recipient an inhibition proportional to the stimulation.

4

This inhibition wears off when the potential mate is seen to be well disposed. As time goes on and the two people

[7] Margaret Mead, *op. cit.*, p. 238 ff.

come into frequent contact, false impressions are corrected and unfounded fears laid to rest. Once an individual ceases to feel that his or her territory is in danger, the source of erotic stimulation will be permitted to come closer, the attraction of this possible mate will be admitted, and the barriers which were erected to forestall a surprise attack or an overwhelming conquest will fall away one by one. As inhibitions break down on both sides, and increasing confidence on one side reduces resistance on the other, the couple will come together and in the end the sex act will take place.

In the following chapters we shall examine all the psychological stages the two parties must go through before this occurs. But for the moment, I would like to take the case of a couple who have been through all this and are leading a normal sex life, e.g., a married couple after the first few months of adjustment, and I would like to ask whether every time they feel desire for one another as the result of the workings of their hormones and their erotic perceptions, they are free from inhibitions. In earlier pages I showed how many internal obstacles there are in the way of stimulation, whether it is produced by close relatives or by strangers. But when the stimulus emanates from a husband or wife, i.e., from someone who is neither a potentially dangerous stranger nor a person forbidden by law or custom, it might well seem that there would be no inhibition at all. If this were so, the analysis I am about to make of the stages leading to the consummation of the sex act would apply neither to lovers nor to married couples. It would apply only to people with little prolonged sexual experience who are still in the preliminary stages. Once these people had achieved intercourse, they would never again suffer from a block in dealing with the erotic excitement their partner arouses.

In practice, however, things do not work this way. Inhibition reappears with every new sexual emotion, and even though repeated experience with the same person gradually makes it decrease, it never disappears altogether. For this to happen, the two partners would have to lose their own identities, and the state of union which is achieved at the moment of the sex act would have to continue after they returned to normal consciousness. This is obviously impossible. The return to a normal state of consciousness in fact implies recovery of separate personalities. Each goes back to his own needs, his own outlook and his own interests. This state of isolation is the normal lot of human beings when not performing the sex act, and it is possible to escape from it only on special occasions—one might almost say at moments of grace—when the barriers that form the Ego have been removed.

While it is a source of untold riches, living with another person is also the cause of much friction. It brings out defects that remained hidden during courtship. It brings out demands far more complex than the superficial needs the partners previously revealed to one another. Before living together, they hardly knew one another and the little they did know was the most superficial part—the part that acts as a facade and buffer to the outside world. This does not mean that either partner had any deliberate intention to cheat or mislead the other. But a person's intimate desires, what could reasonably be called the second half of his personality, become visible to someone else only after they have spent a great deal of time together, and have lived through the moments when long-suppressed anger or discouragement causes the deeper needs of the soul to flare into the open. Circumstances of this sort occur only in the course of living together over many years. The unexpected stresses of life in common reveal the primary and fundamental narcissism of both partners, which breaks through the outer mask of personality and the conventional attitudes imposed by duty or habit.

In one of his most valuable passages, André Breton, true as ever to his high principles, marvels at "the sophistry involved in declaring that the sex act must necessarily be accompanied by a falling off in the partners' capacity for mutual love. This would mean that the very accomplishment of the act of love would bring about its own downfall. Every time an explosion of light burst into life it would be followed by a proportionately darker period of shadow. Each person would thus progressively lose his affinity for any other, would fall back against his will into himself, and in the end would be burnt out by his own brilliance. Love's great soaring would lead sooner or later to the diminution of one partner in the eyes of the other; in the long run other humans would seem more mysterious and more attractive, and both would come back to earth, ready for another choice. It is difficult to imagine anything more insensitive or more soul-destroying than this idea. And no other is so widespread, providing an apt indication of the sorry state of the world today. On this basis, if Juliet had lived, she would not have continued to be ever more essentially Juliet for Romeo."[8]

I am as much amazed as André Breton, but less at people's belief that repeated sex acts must necessarily have a destructive effect on love than at the wear and tear that *in actual fact* affects the sexual and emotional bonds between two people. This is what is really surprising. How is it that two people who have all the time in the world to get to know each other and to study the most recondite secrets of each other's bodies, two people who are apparently able to discover in their mutual abandon a sensual pleasure unattainable anywhere else, do not find that all this continu-

[8] André Breton, *L'Amour fou*, Paris, Gallimard, 1937, pp. 134–135.

ally tightens the bonds between them? It seems to be a terrible exception to the general psychological law which states that any reward or satisfaction leads to repetition of the behavior that produces it, and thus strengthens the ties with the person offering the reward.

Quite rightly, Breton refuses to accept staleness as the explanation of this surprising phenomenon. In so doing, he could have quoted the example of true connoisseurs in any field. Does the wine lover cease to appreciate a wine with which he is familiar? There is of course a pleasure in novelty, but in matters of sex, relations with a new partner must inevitably be less satisfactory than relations with a familiar one—a partner with whom we can lay aside false modesty and of whom we have thorough knowledge, both psychological and physical. Must we then accuse human beings of living a life of illusion in believing that they will find greater satisfaction in the new? Surely not: it is far too easy to attribute everything to imagination. The truth is that it is very difficult for two people living together to satisfy their sexual needs, whether in marriage or not, regardless of the views of those who think that sex life is straightforward and static.

When passion develops between two people, this does not mean that inhibitions disappear. On the contrary, they are likely to increase with time and thus make it more difficult to achieve the abandon which is so necessary for consummation of the sex act. Both partners therefore remain unsatisfied; they hope for new and unusual events to give them back the uninhibited use of their bodies. Obviously if they do try a change, experience will seem to prove them right. What they forget is that the new partner is seen only from the outside, and that they do not have to bring their inner defenses into play. If the affair lasts for any length of time, they will find that all the difficulties and conflicts which made escape from the previous relationship seem desirable will reappear in the new one. Without going into the moral aspects, we may point out that often infidelity occurs because people are unable to overcome a difficulty that sooner or later besets any couple, however well mated and however much in love. This is the problem of narcissism. As long as we deal with others only occasionally and as long as we follow the conventions in our dealings with them, it is relatively easy to bear with their less admirable characteristics. Moreover, we do not see some aspects of their characters at all, and so we are in no position to judge the significance of the unconscious demands these characteristics reflect. If we suddenly get glimpses of the narcissistic dreams of our acquaintances, we do our best to forget them in order to avoid disturbing our social relationships. It is far harder to practice this excellent habit of closing our eyes to the secret motives of others, or of treating them as of no significance, when the people involved are close to us.

Living with another person does far more than bring out each partner's qualities and defects. That would be no great problem. Far more serious is the surfacing of the fears and desires that we call fantasies, which make the inevitable conflicts of daily life so upsetting. A woman who deep down still harbors her childhood dream of being an all-conquering seductress will find it difficult to put up with the ordinariness of her husband, however useful a member of society he may be. Similarly, a man who continues to dream of some mythical virility that enables him to conquer the wildest and most beautiful women will feel threatened by even the merest hint of self-assertion in his wife or mistress. I am not saying that these dreams, with their implied imaginary desires and fears, are dangerous in themselves; but all the same they must be exorcised and their power to dramatize the conflicts of real life must be removed. Particularly at the beginning of life together they are likely to make the partners see each other in a disquieting light. The revelation of unconscious narcissism never fails to engender intense, hardly controllable fear, and to arouse all the instincts of defense. And this is why inhibitions reappear or are strengthened, despite circumstances that seem favorable to erotic stimulation and sexual activities.

As I have shown, all of us are afraid that strangers may attempt to invade our physical and moral territory, in other words, our Ego, and threaten the whole range of emotional links that make up its domain. We still fear the same sort of attack from our partner of a few weeks or months. But now such attacks appear to threaten the very core of our being, and they seem to be launched from the innermost recesses of our partner's personality, thus laying bare his secret narcissism.

André Breton is saddened by the burning up of love, which he sees as evaporating under the effect of repeated sex acts that destroy a partner's mystery and charm. For this he sees only two possible remedies. The first is social, and would consist in leaving the people concerned completely free to choose, thus strengthening passion and love as a hedge against the risks of their exhaustion. The second is moral, and would involve abolishing the "infamous Christian notion of sin," thus making love play so completely innocent that it would no longer be an obstacle to love. "Reciprocated love, as I see it, is a set of mirrors showing me, in a thousand new and mysterious forms, a faithful reflection of my beloved, daily more surprising in its anticipation of my own desires and ever more glowing with life."[9] Breton's analysis and his proposed psychological and social remedies seem to me inadequate. In my view they are still too romantic and too idealistic, in that they fail to recognize the extreme fragility of the sex act, which is

9 *Ibid.*, pp. 136–137.

threatened by quite minor tensions and shows of aggressiveness between even the most passionate partners—and the longer they live together the truer this is.

Love which is fragile to start with will wear out rapidly as the result of a sexual relationship laden with guilt, but even the most innocent sex acts are also inherently fragile and liable to be spoiled by the smallest psychological disturbance. Even if the partners choose each other quite freely and have no feeling of sin in their sexual relations, sooner or later they will come up against each other's narcissism. Then they will have to find a way of exorcising it, of drawing its fangs, if it is not to threaten the perfection of their abandonment in acts of love.

It seems likely that it is failure to overcome this difficulty that prevents many passionate couples from keeping their love alive. As their narcissism is brought to light by many little acts of daily life, the lovers cease to be natural with one another. They begin to feel that they must defend themselves against each other; they do not feel the same pleasure each time they meet, and the charm of being together wears off. Naturally their sexual relations suffer. This defensive attitude affects their bodies and prevents them from relaxing. They become dissatisfied and seek release elsewhere. Neither the emotional nor the sexual relationship has been able to withstand the terrible test of daily life. It is understandable that rather than face this intolerable test, certain lovers wish to die in each other's arms.

For love to be what Breton wants it to be—"a faithful reflection of my beloved, daily more surprising in its anticipation of my own desires and ever more glowing with life"—the conflicts of daily life must be removed and a halt must be called to giving them false meaning. How many husbands return home to find their wife daily more surprising, not in anticipating their desires, but in frustrating them? They see her not ever more glowing with life but disgusted with life and in revolt against it. Breton is not so naive as to be ignorant of this state of affairs. He simply does not seem to have noticed the real difficulty, which is that the lovers must try to avoid becoming frightened or defensive when they perceive their partner's narcissism and private fears, and must remember that these are only temporary manifestations of the imagination, mostly without real significance. Otherwise, their defensive attitudes only widen the gap between them and increase their torment. This is a vicious circle indeed, since the gap leads to the birth of still more narcissistic dreams, and the revelation of these in turn widens the gap still further.

Can this state of affairs be avoided? The difficulties are so great that we cannot expect more than a few couples to be completely successful; but only perfectionists who demand a world peopled by angels should be discouraged by this. Many couples may in fact successfully pass the test of life together, but it is certain that they need to have on their side a whole set of favorable psychological circumstances which enable them first to accept their partner's narcissism and then to go on to exploit it for pleasure, excitement and self-expression. The reader should not be too alarmed by these difficulties, since the rest of this book will be devoted to describing the steps by which lovers can pass from a narcissistic attitude to a more outward-looking one. The important thing to understand is that even when a couple has decided to live together, either in a union approved by society, i.e., in marriage, or in a common-law relationship, their psychological union is not something that can be achieved once and for all. They will still have to fight against deep-seated inhibitions to reach a close-knit and viable union. These inhibitions will not be overcome merely because society approves their living together; they originate in each partner's perception, dim as it may be, of the other's narcissism, and this perception is often confused.

5

So far, the inhibitions encountered at the beginning of any sexual stimulation have been explained by reference to factors arising only from the immediate circumstances of the people concerned, such as social taboos which offset erotic stimuli from near relatives; or the need to protect the Ego and its territory from intrusion and expropriation by strangers or new partners; or a stiffening of attitudes when faced by the narcissism that comes to the surface from time to time even in partners of long standing. In all these cases, the variables arise from the circumstances themselves, and have nothing to do with the past life of the people concerned. If we are to understand the great strength and the universality of inhibitions, we must describe childhood and adolescence at least briefly, since these years must be considered the prehistoric period of any individual's sex life.

What takes us back inevitably to the incidents of childhood is the surprising inhibition we have just observed in partners who know each other well and who have received formal or implicit permission from society to live together. This inhibition is so surprising and unexpected that an explanation based on the latent narcissism of the partners seems incomplete and inadequate. On delving deeper, the sexual psychologist will discover another factor. He will see that bit by bit, and quite without realizing it, either partner may come to see the other as the shadow of a figure from childhood—usually the father or mother.

Every phase of life together is likely to lead a person to make assimilations or comparisons of this sort. To the man, yesterday's fiancée or mistress is now a wife, as his mother was his father's. When the union is blessed with children she becomes a real mother; so much so that, following a custom which tells us a great deal about this assimilation process, many husbands call their wives by the same name ("Mother") that the children use. This may be only a detail but it does at least throw light on the tendency of husbands to identify themselves with children and to find substitute mothers in their wives.

Is the situation very different for women? Although it is more complex, it follows the same rules. From the day the man becomes a husband and father, the woman begins to assimilate him to her own father. But at a still deeper level, her husband's smiles, or ways of making fun of her, or reassuring her, or caressing her—all have a maternal meaning; and sometimes the wife quite unconsciously turns her husband into a mother figure. At this level, the relationship of wife to husband is like that of husband to wife; both of them beg or try to beg for maternal gestures and behavior, but both are afraid of meeting a rebuff.

As soon as there is the slightest unconscious assimilation of a partner to a parental figure, the taboos of childhood come to the surface again. Among these is the fundamental ban on incest, so strong whenever erotic stimulation arose from father or mother; later on, if either spouse becomes a father or a mother figure, he or she will appear as a forbidden object.

We have already noted how surprising it is that so many couples find each other less attractive the longer they live together. The partial explanation I gave earlier may now be completed by introducing the notion of an educational process: the replacement of the early physical intimacy of the newborn child with its mother by the looser ties of family life. In adult life people live through the same sequence of events, moving from physical intimacy to mere family relationships. The early months of intense physical pleasure, similar to that experienced by a newborn child in its mother's arms, are followed by a period when these joys lose their charm, as if the couple were being weaned. The result is that the partners now live on friendly terms like brother and sister, or like children with their parents.

The history of many couples appears very much like a repetition of the sequence of events that marks the beginning of human life: symbiosis followed by weaning and separation, leaving only a degree of familiarity lying midway between carnal intimacy and spiritual friendship. Finding themselves in this situation, which is the normal relationship between children and parents, many partners regret their inability to achieve the new and deeper intimacy to be found in a true sexual relationship, and suffer from their failure to do so.

What causes this inability? All the earlier prohibitions whose purpose was to prevent the degeneration of familiarity into overt sexual behavior. This is the first and most obvious meaning of the Oedipus and pre-Oedipus conflicts described by psychoanalysts. It would be quite wrong to consider these conflicts in the same light as those that arise in normal, fully developed adult sex life, as if a son's attachment to his mother or a daughter's to her father were an outright sexual relationship conducted in the face of opposition from a rival to be fought off or killed. While all the conflicts of adult sex life cast their shadows before them during childhood, in early life sexual tendencies are always stifled in one way or another to prevent the family unit from closing in on itself under the sexual domination of father or mother. Each individual therefore emerges from childhood with a whole set of inhibitions.

What is unique about the biological growth of human beings is that the environment within which the individuals struggle for survival is a tightly knit family. For this reason, each person builds up a set of positive and negative attitudes which subconsciously govern his adult contacts with people from other social groups, and often prevent him from adapting himself to the outside world. Such is the power of psychological determinism. At the age when the sex organs reach the point of development at which, in the absence of obstacles, boys and girls would try to have sexual relationships, they already have certain attitudes, favorable or unfavorable, toward the opposite sex as such. Earlier experiences—some agreeable, some unpleasant— have led them to develop their own personalities; they are not simply empty rooms available for occupancy by the first attractive mate to come along. Moreover, the attitudes may themselves be overlaid by stereotyped images arising from an often one-sided and subjective interpretation of parental behavior. It is through these long-lasting images that people perceive the men and women who come into their field of vision. In short, the sex instinct does not develop in a vacuum. When it finally reaches the light of day as the result of the physiological changes of puberty and adolescence, it is absorbed into an already existing system of attitudes and images.

Husbands or wives are not the only ones who are seen through the screen of images people create for themselves from observing their parents' behavior. Any possible mate is automatically endowed with the features of one of the members of the childhood family. As these relatives were usually associated with behavior bans, anyone assimilated to them will be associated with similar bans, especially when the new relationship is a socially acceptable one; and the more the mates are like the parents, the stronger this effect will be.

This explains, at least in part, why some men permit themselves to have sexual relations with common or loose women who cannot by any stretch of the imagination be likened to their mother, while they become sexually paralyzed in the presence of any woman who reminds them of her: she is, after all, the person with whom they passed their childhood years, forbidden the opportunity to express their desire for her.

We must be careful not to underestimate the importance of the system of attitudes and images which we inherit from our childhoods and which tends to fix our later attitude to both the opposite sex and our own. This system is not merely or necessarily an obstacle to satisfactory adjustment to other people, and indeed it has a useful function. The human race is revealed to us through fathers and mothers, who are, after all, similar to all the other men and women in the world, and so our relations with our parents can form a reasonable basis for our relations with other people. If we fit in well in our own family environment, this is a good augury for adaptation to adult life, and I am very far from decrying the influence of our youth. I have emphasized the importance of the events of childhood and the attitudes and images that it leaves in our mind and imagination, not to deplore them, but to draw attention to one of the major causes of inhibition affecting the early stages of erotic excitement. Taken all in all, this inhibition is not very serious for most people. On the contrary, without it the erotic stimulation would trigger the whole sexual cycle on the spot, and the process would take place rapidly, but without any particular pleasure. The human race probably derives its best qualities from the tension arising from the conflict between stimulation and inhibition.

Having come to the end of my analysis of the causes of the inhibitions holding erotic stimuli in check, I am prepared for a certain number of objections. The first that comes to mind is the one-sided nature of my analysis. I shall certainly be told that in studying the psychological state of an individual receiving erotic stimuli I have looked only at the negative factors, that is, those that impede the spontaneous development of sexual feeling in the human body. It will be said that I have ignored both the strength and the nature of sex stimuli, which may be a veritable tidal wave, sweeping away all the defenses an individual has erected to protect himself.

I can answer this objection quite briefly. My purpose in spending so much time describing the various causes of inhibition—some of them deep-seated, some superficial— is not to deny the power of erotic excitement, but, since this can be taken for granted, to draw attention to the phenomenon of inhibition, which is less well known. It may be one of the side effects of the egocentric nature of mankind that people are quicker to recognize the strength of their instincts than of the obstacles they themselves put in the way. They tend to consider these obstacles to a normal sex life as something quite outside their control, and as having no effect on the primary force of their sex instinct. They are loath to believe that inhibitions, which are caused by social taboos or by the real or imagined hesitations of their potential partner, enter into the erotic stimulus itself and serve not to suppress it but to pervert it in a way that I shall shortly describe. The battles for the human soul, especially those concerned with sex, are not fought only in the border areas of the self where it comes in contact with the outside world, nor are they straightforward struggles between the spontaneous forces of the soul and external enemies bent on their destruction. They also take place within the individual himself, and the mainspring of his personality is affected by the outside forces. His whole being is pulled this way and that by erotic stimuli and inhibitions. Perhaps one day we shall discover the ways in which stimuli and inhibitions work in opposite directions simultaneously within the higher animals, just as we already know about the stimuli and inhibitions that have external origins. A discovery of this sort would be in line with the pattern of opposites now being revealed by phys-

iologists in many fields of research, which have recently
given us anabolism and catabolism, sympathetic stimulation and parasympathetic inhibition, stimulating hormones
and paralyzing hormones.

A second objection that might be made to my analysis is
one of method. I shall be told that I have no right to treat
excitement and inhibition so differently, that in dealing
with excitement I have merely assumed an unconscious
physical stimulus, while to make a case for inhibition I
have brought in complicated psychological facts and situations (moral and physical territory, the Ego, perception of
narcissism in partners, etc.) which assume a considerable
past history. It will be put to me that I should remember
that any erotic stimulus is also affected from the earliest
moment by all past experience. A purely physical erotic
stimulus, the objector will say, is an abstraction which does
not fit the whole array of facts.

I agree that I have treated stimulation and inhibition
differently, and I will repeat in justification what I said in
reply to the first objection. At the beginning of this study
the important thing was not to describe the various forms
of erotic excitement, but to throw light on the many causes
which prevent it from being spontaneous, which compel
it to go into hiding and make it assume a number of different forms. Without inhibition, there would be nothing
to say about sexual excitement. It would set off spontaneous physical reactions, but it would never take on the complex forms in which we know it. That is why it was important to start by throwing light on the phenomenon of
inhibition.

I am so impressed with the complexity of the forms of
erotic stimulation in human beings that the whole of the
rest of this book is devoted to explaining how they work.
But in order to give a plausible account of the psychological complexities connected with them, I had first to ex-

plain why stimulation has to undergo so many changes before the sex act can be achieved. All these reasons can be summarized in one word: inhibition.

I would give the same reply to the final objection that I foresee, which is that I have not taken into account the psychological inhibition that is inherent in erotic stimulation as such. By this I mean that many people feel that such stimulation is dangerous for themselves, for the other party, or for both. They have a vague idea that it will release alarming forces which may destroy both the person from whom it emanates and the person to whom it is directed. Of course I am familiar with this idea that sex is a destructive force. But for me the interesting thing is to discover how this fantasy arose and why it continually recurs in the human mind. I will only repeat that without the phenomenon of inhibition, erotic stimulation would occur freely, even more or less automatically as with animals, without ever acquiring the demoniac and dramatic force that it has with some people, and indeed with all people at certain stages of their psychological development.

For the rest of this book, therefore, I shall be concerned with the transformations undergone by simple erotic stimulation under the pressure of inhibitions. This in itself is a tribute to the unshatterable force that I believe this stimulation to possess. No taboos ever suppress it completely, for it overcomes obstacles by taking the most unexpected forms.

II

SEXUALITY AND AGGRESSION: PERVERSE TENDENCIES

Since it is reasonable to define a chain reaction by its final term, we may consider the whole course of sexual relations as the sum of all those movements by which two beings come together, touch and stimulate one another until they achieve a paroxysm like rejuvenation, which represents the high point of vital tension.

In order to understand the various stages of sexual contact, we must assume as a working hypothesis that two parallel series of reactions take place in living organisms: one leading to the paralysis, dismemberment and death of a prey or enemy; the other to the life-giving, rejuvenating stimulation of a partner. The former leads to aggression, the latter to sexual activity. The two are entirely different in their end results, which are, theoretically at least, the annihilation of life and a life-giving paroxysm, respectively. In practice, things are not so clearly separated. We shall see that at the beginning of sex life, just because of the ambiguities and contradictions of the state of simultaneous inhibition and stimulation, the two series of reactions are intermingled, at least at the elementary level, thus creating what psychologists call tendencies to perversion, which are in fact strange and sometimes frightening mixtures of sexual activity and aggression.

Many laboratory experiments have shown that frustration produces aggression. For example, when a need is created or awakened in individuals (often children) for which no satisfaction is possible, the result is a substantial increase in destructive impulses. Of course, we all know how a hungry dog reacts when it is first offered sugar and then denied it; these reactions are very violent and take the form of a kind of rage that drives the animal to bite anything within reach.

If frustration is defined as a state in which the individual is simultaneously stimulated and inhibited, attracted in a particular direction and then prevented from acting on the attraction, it is clear that in matters of sex human beings have good reason to feel frustrated. The whole purpose of the preceding chapter was to show that erotic stimulation, which makes one person wish to draw close to another, always starts by coming up against barriers that prevent the forces generated from being freely released.

But the resulting changes in these forces are not so much changes in direction as in kind. An inhibited person is still drawn toward an attractive individual. But he will not wish to stimulate or caress her and lead her to a paroxysm of tenderness; instead he will wish to attack, hurt and even destroy her. The dynamic has changed; from being a positive force which favors the attractive individual, it becomes negative and destructive.

We should, however, be wary of thinking of the process as one in which erotic forces are quite simply replaced by aggressive and destructive ones. The aggressiveness which occurs in these circumstances is not as firm or clear-cut as that which arises in a person called upon to defend his territory, alone or with others. Far from being a healthy combativeness designed to meet real external dangers, it retains certain erotic elements from its frustrated sexual origin. It is directed toward a deeply needed human being, and this fundamental ambivalence gives the aggressive impulse an erotic character, and makes the erotic stimulation aggressive. It is this confusion, almost organic in nature, between erotic and aggressive forces that I shall call the perverse tendency.

In the history of the study of perversions, Freud was the first who was not content with mere description but began to look for an explanatory theory. Starting with a study of sexual deviations and neuroses, he first discovered that neuroses always conceal latent sexual deviations and thus that "neuroses are, so to say, the negative of perversions."[1] Going on to seek the origin of perversions, he began to examine children, and on the basis of psychoanalysis and naive observation of children's behavior, he came to the conclusion that without exception they all had tendencies to sexual perversion. This is the meaning of the second part of the well-known title *Three Essays on the Theory of Sexuality: Various Forms of Perversion in Children*. This does not mean that children are bound to commit vicious acts, or that what would be vicious in adults would be equally so in children. Freud's work has often been misinterpreted, and not enough attention has been paid to the distinction that he makes between actual perversion, which results in overt acts, and a tendency—*eine Anlage, eine Veranlagung*—to perverse behavior, which comes to the surface in children only when they fall under the sway of abnormal seductive influences. What appears naturally in children is the tendency.

[1] Sigmund Freud, *Three Essays on the Theory of Sexuality*, London, The Hogarth Press and the Institute of Psycho-Analysis, 1962, p. 31.

I shall not attempt to discuss Freud's views on the origins of sexual neurosis or on the perverse nature of sexuality in infants. The former are for psychiatrists, and the latter for developmental psychologists, and so neither comes within the scope of this book. But in Freud's work there are some statements of general principle which are usually ignored, because they are considered either self-evident or unimportant. For example, on several occasions, and often at the end of a long analysis, Freud asserts that he cannot help but recognize, in the predisposition to all forms of perversion, the "original, universal characteristic of the human sex instinct." Making use of an even stronger and more concise expression, he declares that these tendencies belong to the very nature of man himself (*das allgemein Menchliche und Ursprungliche*).[2]

Everything hinges on what is meant by *das Ursprungliche,* the original thing, i.e., what is "original." It is usual to consider that the author meant to use the word in a developmental, and hence a chronological, sense. Taking this view, "original" would apply to something that comes first in a person's history, in the early stages of childhood. And yet, the preceding general statements hint at a more far-reaching meaning, according to which "original" means something elemental or fundamental, something that comes to the fore when sexual needs well up, regardless of whether the people concerned are children or adults. If this interpretation is accepted, in the field of sexuality "original human nature" would mean the primary manifestations of the sex instinct, whether or not they have their roots in the earliest years of life.

In the next few pages, I shall try to show that it is reasonable to believe that the tendencies to perversion appear, if not at the beginning of human existence, at least at the

[2] *Ibid.*

very start of sex life as such. If this can be proved, we may infer that tendencies to perversion also occur in children when sexual development takes place. But as we have agreed to limit this study to erotic stimulation in persons who are physiologically adult, we shall omit some of the developmental considerations and concentrate on the primary forms taken by fully developed sexual instincts when they come up against inhibitions.

These primary forms may be called demoniacal, if by "demoniacal" we mean an inextricable confusion of good and evil in such a way that good becomes evil and vice versa, and there is no distinction between the two. In the form of perversion generally called vice, erotic tension, which is good in itself, becomes aggressive, and aggressive impulses become erotic. It would be unwise or even dangerous to try to conceal the existence of this demoniacal force, which exists in the very depths of the soul behind a facade of reassuring illusions. It is only by bringing it into the light that it can be identified and exorcised.

1

It has become standard practice to divide sexual aberrations into two groups, depending on whether the departure from the normal relates to the object of desire or to the goal pursued. The first group describes people who are sexually stimulated by seeing not an adult mate of the opposite sex, but an inanimate object with a strong erotic appeal (fetishism connected with hair, feet, etc.), or a child (pederasty), or an adult partner of the same sex (homosexuality). The second group describes people who find sexual pleasure only in the mouth, the anus or some part of the body other than the genital organs, or who like to show themselves in the nude or to see others in the nude (exhi-

bitionism or voyeurism), or who inflict pain on themselves
or on others (masochism or sadism).

For the time being we shall put aside the first group. As
it involves an error in the spontaneous choice of a mate, it
cannot be properly understood until enough inner changes
have occurred in the original erotic stimulation to bring
it to bear on some object, either a person or thing. But we
can certainly discuss the second group straightaway.

It is tempting to start by making a fundamental distinction between aberrations which arise simply from the
erogenous nature of any part of the body that has nerves,
and those which are caused by an urge to seek pleasure in
suffering. At first glance there would seem to be a clear-cut
distinction between the two, for while any kind of casual
stimulation forms a natural preparation for normal sexual
behavior, the erotic pleasure that some people find in cruelty can only be called abnormal and perverted.

But this judgment is too black and white. If we look
more closely, we shall see that a distinction can be made
only at the end of the sexual cycle. We say, for example,
that the pleasures derived from certain parts of the body
are less abnormal because they fit into the cycle leading to
copulation. But although we can make a distinction between sexual behavior in which all the erogenous parts of
the body are exploited for enjoyment, and sadistic or masochistic behavior in which pain is the basis of pleasure, we
would be wrong to make the same distinction with regard
to the origins of sexual excitement. In fact, the distinction
occurs in a very late phase of the individual's sexual development. In the early stages, erotic stimulation is less
specialized, and is experienced in the nongenital parts of
the body; for this very reason it contains the germs of aggressiveness, sadism or masochism.

The theories of psychoanalysts have not always succeeded in explaining the very great difference between the

pleasures derived from the different parts of the body in a normal, completed sex act, and those same pleasures at the beginning of the individual's sexual development. Once adult partners have succeeded in overcoming their aggressiveness toward one another, they give themselves to each other wholeheartedly and every part of the body plays a positive role. Each tries to excite the other to the very limits of pleasure. The diffuse erogenous nature of the body is used for purposes of love. But this takes place only at the end of a long process involving the slow diminution of aggressiveness.

Conversely, at the beginning of sexual excitement, the inhibitions that are thrown up and the resulting nervous tension of the whole body make the stimulation aggressive in a way that is not inherent in the process itself. For, the state of nervous excitement seems to affect first the parts of the body particularly adapted for self-preservation. At the end of the process, the balance is reversed and the erotic stimulation becomes strong enough to impart feelings of love to the entire body. This is a qualitative difference which makes it reasonable to say that at least at the beginning of sex life, the general erogenous nature of the body is closely related to aggressive tendencies, that is to say, to tendencies which if they persisted too long would lead in the later phases to masochistic or sadistic behavior.

When erotic excitement is inhibited, a sort of displacement occurs. Instead of developing in the genital organs, the tension spreads to the rest of the body, and especially to those parts devoted to self-defense and contact with other people, i.e., the mouth, the eyes, the anus and the muscles of the arms and legs. It must be emphasized that most of these organs and muscles have aggressive or defensive functions quite apart from any erotic role they may play.

To show this, I shall start with the mouth, the organ which plays a primary role in self-preservation and shapes our first encounters with the outside world. It is worth noting that the term most generally used both philosophically and psychologically to describe a person's tendencies is the word "appetite." For example, we speak of sexual appetite as if the mate were an object of prey to be mastered and eaten. It should also be noted that the act of eating is the act of destruction par excellence. That is why erotic excitement tends to become destructive if it is concentrated too exclusively in the mouth.

I know that I shall be asked, What about kissing, which is the the tenderest expression of love between humans? I agree that kissing plays an essential and useful role in expressing love between human beings, at least in Western society. But it does so only when the mouth has given up its aggressive functions of seizing, biting and swallowing, and by a paradox, begins to serve a function which is precisely opposite its natural one; and so when people kiss, they are prepared to feed their mates on their own substance. The kiss is a victory over destructive appetite. In an act of daring found in mankind alone, the kiss makes use of the primary organ of destruction to express subordination and self-surrender. But I repeat that this reversal of the natural functions is the result of a long process of change. Originally, sex acts concentrated on the mouth represent the desire to swallow a prey which has received sexual significance from the primary erotic stimulus. This explains fantasies like those in which people see the female vagina as a mouth or the mouth as a vagina with teeth; it explains the fear of making an attractive partner bleed by biting too fiercely, or of being eaten up and swallowed by a too-pressing admirer.

The second important function connecting an individual to the outside world is the passing of excrement or residues out of the human body in the form of feces and urine. I believe Saint Augustine was the first person to express surprise that the function of procreation should take place *inter urinam et faeces.* But there is really nothing shocking in this. Because the organs are close together, people tend to associate one function with the other, thus making it easy to confuse a noble, life-giving secretion with a necessary excretion of dead substances.

I would like to point out that excretion is an aggressive act not only because it was the subject of rigid rules in childhood, but also because it involves passing something that has no further value out of the body. This is what makes it an insult to call someone "crap," for it is a way of saying that he means nothing, and should be gotten out of the way as fast as possible. This, too, is why it is considered an insult to call someone by any name that is a synonym for those substances everybody wants to get out of their system. If you analyze language, you will find that every attitude of rejection is expressed in terms of evacuation, i.e., vomiting, pissing or shitting. As erotic stimulation occurs *inter urinam et faeces,* it is easy to understand how it takes on an aggressive, coarse and repugnant meaning.

In general, clinical observation shows that the more hostile a person's relations are with the opposite sex, the more will his sexual ideas be concentrated on the anus; they will be expressed in images in which both the emission of seed by a man and the birth of a child from a woman are symbolized in terms of excretion.

It would take too long to describe all the psychological problems caused by the confusion between procreation and excretion in the early stages of sex life. I only want to emphasize here that sexually speaking, individuals are not psychologically mature until they are not only logically but emotionally capable of distinguishing the life-giving cells and bodily union from excrement and its removal from the body. Until this differentiation is made spontaneously, the sex act will still be felt to be connected with urinating and defecating, and thus will contain the element of aggressiveness which is inherent in the preservation of life by the elimination of dead substances.

Actions resulting in the incorporation of food substances in the body and those connected with the evacuation of excrement both belong to the category of acts necessary for survival, and are thus basic to the struggle for life. To use them for pleasure is bound to introduce an element of conflict. By becoming involved with sex, the instinctive actions connected with self-preservation temporarily change their functional role for one of pleasure and relaxation. But in so doing they inevitably pass on to sexual activities some of their own aggressive content.

Much the same thing must be said about another vital function: sight. In the normal process of growing up, is not the first use of the eyes to help supply the mouth? It is by using its eyes that an animal picks out the creatures that are likely to threaten its food or its life, and selects the things that it can use for nourishment.

While the sense of smell, to which too little attention has so far been paid by sex psychologists, is probably linked with the need for contact with mates of the same species, vision seems to be related more closely to the instinct of self-defense. Vigilance, wakefulness, watchfulness, keeping a weather eye out are all attitudes involving the use of sight for the discovery of food or defense against hidden enemies. Only secondarily, and after stimulation through the sense of smell, does sight seem to play a part in finding a mate or its genital organs. It is perhaps also significant that the eyes usually close spontaneously at the moment when feelings of passion are at their height, as if the lovers wished to lower their defenses and abolish any distance between them.

Only when the sex act is about to take place, i.e., when most of the barriers have been overcome, does the gaze become languid, in harmony with an attitude of surrender. The eyes remain open just enough to suggest an act that would close them in sexual pleasure. A popularly accepted way of inviting a suitable partner to join in a sex act is by winking. This is a way of using the eyes, as in other more suggestive means of seduction, to indicate that the individual is prepared to forego any offensive or defensive action. The eyes have relaxed their usual vigilance. By this, I mean that sight is normally connected with self-preservation, the defense of a person's territory or goods, and the search for food. By pretending to close them, a person is saying that he is willing to give up the perpetual struggle to preserve his identity against all comers.

Voyeurs' eyes are always strained by the search for sexual prey, and they reflect the hope of paralyzing it once found. Strictly speaking, voyeurism is a transitory phenomenon, since the eyes are being used for sexual pursuit instead of for the pursuit of food. In this intermediate state, the eyes, although fixed on the outside world, are not fully given over to it because of the desire for internal pleasures, which require withdrawal from the world. It is this which gives to voyeurs' faces a peculiarly equivocal expression which is a sure sign of perversion.

Exhibitionism, the active form of voyeurism, is just as aggressive a phenomenon. The purpose of the exhibitionist is to arouse a feeling of sexual discomfort in the spectator, who is often despised or denigrated. Certainly, there is an element of brutality in this showing off of one's body to a stranger, if only because the aim is to provoke sexual greed, in which an appetite for destruction is mixed with the desire for satisfaction.

When a harmonious sex act successfully follows a period of mutual adjustment, sight plays an important role as a stimulus. At this point, it has lost the aggressive element stemming from its primary connection with the functions

of self-preservation and acquisition. But at the beginning
of sexual stimulation, everybody's eyes behave like those of
voyeurs or exhibitionists because in all sexual activities
there is some element of desire to devour the mate.

When the partners are not truly in harmony, the periods
of separation are also times when the eyes again become
avid and aggressive, like those of voyeurs or exhibitionists,
just as in the early stages of sex relations.

What parts of the body are of greatest interest to this
avid gaze? Naturally the reproductive organs, the *phallus*
and the *vulva*. This is at least a partial explanation of what
psychoanalysts call the castration complex. Because of this
greedy gaze cast upon the sex organs, the mate feels threatened, and is especially afraid that these particular organs
may be harmed. To explain this fear we need not invoke
earlier threats of real castration. The aggressive attitude
and the concupiscent glances of both partners are sufficient
to explain their fears for their intimate parts. Undoubtedly,
this kind of fear does occur in childhood, since even then
sexual feelings are present, but real fear of this sort is
closely associated with mature sexuality and is, indeed, its
natural consequence, since sexuality starts by making itself felt through the organs of self-preservation and acquisition, and thus includes an aggressive element which it
will take some time to shed.

This fear for the sex organs gives rise to an overestima-
tion of their importance, which explains most of the com-
pulsive masturbatory habits adopted by people whose circumstances or inhibitions prevent them from carrying
erotic stimulation to a normal, successful conclusion. But
whatever the final outcome of the stimulation, there is
always a phase in which the sex organs receive special attention, either from oneself or one's partner, a phase intended first of all to calm the fears born of earlier aggres-

sive sexual attitudes and then to lead on from excitement to the final paroxysm of intercourse.

The transformation of erotic excitement into aggressiveness also tends to occur in connection with the muscles used in daily life to fight off a rival or overcome a recalcitrant mate.

Since an attractive partner may be jealously guarded or pursued by other individuals, a certain degree of combativeness will be required if he or she is to be conquered and possessed. The sex game is never played out between a male and a female in isolation from the rest of the world; there is always a triangular situation, for whenever a male approaches a female he must be prepared to take on any genuine rival. The literature on animal behavior abounds in examples of struggles between individuals of the same sex. Tinbergen stresses the close connection between sexual and combative behavior in animals: a male finding himself near a female in his own territory is likely to attack any other animal who might be a rival.[3] In general, "visible behavior of a threatening nature is also designed to attract females."[4] Again, analyzing the behavior of the herring gull, Tinbergen notes that the first sign of sexual excitement is aggressiveness toward others.[5] Among songbirds he found an even closer connection, for the male's song both attracts the females and drives off the males.[6] In the animal world whenever there is competition for the conquest of sexual mates, even the simplest sexual stimulation seems to set off simultaneously behavior that attracts mates (sexuality) and behavior that drives other individuals away (ag-

[3] N. Tinbergen, *The Study of Instinct,* Oxford, Clarendon, 1955, p. 177.

[4] *Ibid.,* p. 182.

[5] N. Tinbergen, *The Herring Gull's World,* London, Collins, 2nd ed., 1960, p. 121.

[6] N. Tinbergen, *The Study of Instinct, supra,* p. 178.

gressiveness). In fact, competition seems to create a state of acute excitement that is both erotic and aggressive.

From a logical or rational standpoint, it would seem obvious that among human beings at least, aggressiveness would be directed toward rivals and gestures of sexual intention toward an attractive potential mate. But such a distinction implies that it is possible to differentiate immediately between potential mates and others. In the early stages, this is not so; the perceptual system is quite unaware of external distinctions, and sex-oriented behavior is automatically accompanied by compensating aggressive behavior.

Moreover, even behavior designed to attract a mate contains some element of aggression. For biological or psychological reasons the desired mate may well take flight; the steps required to prevent it involve aggressive behavior, calling for the use of the same legs, arms and hands as are required for seizing or overwhelming an enemy; and if resistance continues after the potential mate has been overpowered, the sex act will take the form of rape, the very epitome of sexual aggressiveness. If the female yields, the male's movements become gentler and turn into caresses intended to stimulate the whole body, but more especially the pelvic muscles, as this will facilitate copulation.

To sum up, we can say that when individuals remain separated by the conventions of daily life and by personal taste, despite the sexual attraction that may exist between them, erotic stimulation will automatically bring on stimulation of the organs connected with consumption, excretion, attraction and conquest. In fact, it really seems as if the purposes of erotic stimulation can only be achieved and all the obstacles overcome if all the aggressive parts of the body are first brought into play.

Is this really only an unfounded assumption? It is true that so far physiologists who have studied the nervous system have not produced proofs in its favor, but neither have they denounced it. While awaiting the outcome of further work on sexual physiology, we should at least pay attention to the findings of ethology—the study of animal behavior —and psychoanalysis—the study of human mental behavior—which appear to tend in the same direction. The ethologists put considerable stress on the frequency of what they call displacement activities, in which opposite reactions are often involved; the psychoanalysts have reported many fantasies in which erotic tendencies take the form of aggressiveness involving the mouth, the anus, the eyes or the limbs. All I have done is to try to give a plausible explanation of this perverse structure—a mixture of aggression and sex—which arises in the early stages of stimulation as a result of the obstacles that stand in the way of following up on it.

This means that in the early stages of a sexual relationship, the relationship between the two individuals is very ambiguous. On the one hand, they are linked by the erotic signals that flow naturally between them, while on the other hand, they are held apart by all their instincts of self-defense and self-preservation. This confusion produces aggressiveness in sexual behavior, and if this behavior keeps to its original pattern and does not evolve into something that can provide greater satisfaction for the individuals or for the species, it will erupt into acts in which aggression provides the main source of pleasure. As a result, the relationship will be one-sided, as all human relationships tend to be, and so one partner will have an active and sadistic role, while the other will be content with the passive and masochistic one. But in a normal relationship, the sadistic and masochistic elements will drop out, leaving sexual desire to triumph finally over aggressiveness, and each partner will try to give the other greater pleasure by using the full range of sensual experience.

2

Although they are often placed in situations where they are simultaneously stimulated and inhibited, all adults do not become perverts, and it is for this reason that we must speak only of tendencies to perversion. In some people these tendencies are very strong, or circumstances favor them, and lead to overt acts or particular behavior patterns. In most people, however, they do not come to the surface, but are buried by a mental process that I shall describe shortly.

In order to leave room for individual differences I have used the term "perverse tendency." The state of combined stimulation and inhibition does not necessarily lead to perverse acts, but it does set up a tendency in that direction. In the most extreme cases this tendency comes to the surface unmodified and leads to the behavior known as perversion or vice; in normal circumstances it is inhibited, just as is the original erotic stimulation.

Perverse tendencies vary from one person to another. Some people will have a strong oral tendency, and so erotic stimulation will be likely to take the form of aggressive action related to the taking in of food. Others will have an anal tendency, and so erotic stimulation will be concentrated in the nerves and muscles controlling excretion and urination. Still others will have a tendency toward combativeness, and erotic excitement will be closely bound up with a desire to drive off a rival. The causes of these different tendencies are doubtless to be found in the makeup of the individuals themselves and in their early childhood traumatic experiences.

It is the job of psychiatrists and psychologists to study those cases in which an original perverse tendency is so powerful that it makes the individual act in accordance with its dictates. In this book, however, we are not concerned with actual perversion; our concern is with normal sexual behavior. Nevertheless, we should not ignore perversions altogether; they are always present as a threat which is usually more or less successfully held at bay.

Why and how does an individual overcome this threat? What are his reasons for countering the perverse tendencies aroused by combined stimulation and inhibition, and in what way does he do it?

I see two main reasons why these original tendencies are inhibited: First, the body is torn by conflicting impulses toward destructive aggression and erotic stimulation, and so it must undergo an almost unbearable torment causing great anxiety. It will therefore, whenever possible, instinctively seek some other course of action. It is only when these other outlets are unduly limited that it will seek escape from the intolerable tension in perverse behavior. Second, as perverse action implies an element of intense aggressiveness, the individual may fear retaliation by the partner he is tempted to attack. If he is convinced that aggression will always be met by equal aggression, he will suppress his tendencies in the same way he suppresses expressions of bad temper.

How will he set about doing this? It will surely not be sufficient merely to run away from the sources of erotic excitement. Not only is a flight of this sort impossible, since there are potential mates everywhere, but it would deprive him of all the benefits of social existence. The problem is thus one of offsetting the erotic emotions generated by potential partners without running away from them, and this can only be done by working on the perverse tendencies while they are still in the mind. It is more important to control the tendencies than to run away from their causes.

If a human being were capable of controlling all his physical impulses in a rational fashion, he would, when faced by a sexually attractive partner, take care straightaway to separate aggressive instincts from erotic ones, and keep only the latter. But human beings do not have absolute control over their impulses. Particularly at the beginning of sex life, the mind is not sufficiently alert to discover the difference between aggressiveness and sex. The earliest sexual feelings give rise to tendencies that are far more like involuntary reactions than genuine impulses. In these confused reactions characteristic of early love affairs there is as much aggression as there is love, and it is virtually impossible to separate the good from the bad.

That one should avoid temptation by avoiding people who are sexually stimulating is a commonplace. But any individual can become a source of erotic feeling and create disturbances in parts of the body that have become sensitive to outside stimuli. As flight is by no means always appropriate, all that can be done is to make the body insensitive to outside erotic stimuli. The usual name for this operation is "desexualization"; it is also described as withdrawal of libido when faced by conscious or unconscious advances by possible mates.

The simplest method of doing this is to shift the target of the impulse, and to replace the person who is the real cause both of the excitement and the inhibition, but whom it would be fatal to subject to erotic aggressiveness, by more inoffensive objects. This is called displacement or substitute activity, and is one of the most elementary defense mechanisms known to man. The perverse impulse will show itself in acts directed not at its actual target but at objects having some similarity to it. This mechanism can best be illustrated by reference to children and their apparent cruelty. Ants, cats, dogs, dolls and many other objects are displacement victims, receiving the blows which cannot be administered to father, mother or some other member of the family. But we would be showing character-

istic adult blindness to consider that such actions are performed only by children or, when they are observed in
adults, to attribute them entirely to childhood circumstances. It would be more accurate to say that the state of
simultaneous sexual excitement and inhibition in itself
creates perverse impulses which an adult normally diverts
from their natural course by directing them against ideas,
political parties or institutions—in brief, against impersonal and inoffensive enemies that are really the adult's
equivalent of dolls and substitute victims. Of course, it
would be too easy to explain the moral and occasionally
physical vandalism of adults merely by ascribing such behavior to sexual frustration and the displacement mechanism, but clinical observation shows that ill-balanced sexuality does enter into it.

It is certainly the capacity for substitution, such a striking feature of the flexibility of the human mind, that explains much of the peculiar behavior observed in people
when they fall in love. We should normally expect them to
show sympathy for everything and everyone connected
with the loved one; we should, for example, expect a man
to praise his beloved's family. Yet things do not go as
smoothly as that. Very often all that we hear is criticism of
her father, brothers or sisters. Is not this aggressive behavior simply a manifestation of the desire to tear her away
from her family, a reply to the possessive instinct that most
lovers recognize in their beloved's family, as if the family
would refuse to give up one of its members to an outsider?
But if the wooer's sole purpose were to gain possession of
the desired one, he would set about it more skillfully, by
playing upon the generosity of her relatives. In fact, his behavior closely resembles a substitute activity, by which
erotic aggressiveness is shifted from its natural target—the
desired person—to members of his or her group, whom it
is possible to attack without coming to blows. This particu-

lar substitution is relatively innocuous, since the wooer can often count upon support from the beloved, who will thus also discharge aggressive tendencies on members of the family.

One case of substitution deserves special attention. This is when an individual turns against himself the impulses he cannot discharge on anyone else. He is not choosing a harmless external object, but his own body. In human beings the earliest manifestation of this self-centered displacement is well known: it is that of the baby who seeks to find a substitute for its mother's breast by sucking its own thumb. Perverse tendencies in adults lead to more complex self-centered substitutions, but the principle is the same.

Thus, what was originally sadism may turn into masochism. Attempts will be made to inflict erotic cruelty not on the person of the beloved but on the body of the lover himself, who will find pleasure in self-inflicted torments. A certain number of self-mutilations both by children and by adults come into this category. When adults masturbate, this in many cases represents a desire to suck the erotic parts turned back upon the person's own body. And even the perverse desire to engage in anal insertion may, if foiled, lead to wanting to have this act performed on oneself.

These self-centered perversions may appear at the beginning of sex life, or even later if sexual experience is unsatisfactory. Under the stimulus of sexual excitement a person may masturbate or torture himself morally or physically. In order to prevent the perverse tendency from leading to an attack on the source of the stimulation, an individual may as a safety measure substitute himself and, in secrecy to avoid any risk of criticism, perform on his own body the acts he cannot perform with someone else. This is a subtle and instinctive device enabling him to avoid carrying out perverse acts on an unknown person who would certainly be badly frightened and try to escape either by running away or by a violent counteroffensive, both of which reactions he naturally wishes to avoid.

Whether the specific target of the perverse tendency is replaced by the individual's own body or by some other object—animal or thing—makes no difference: in both cases a perversion actually takes place. In these conditions, where action is deflected from its specific target, there is no real mental attempt to work on the perverse tendency; behavior is expressed in action and bursts out into real life. There is very little progress, if by "progress" we mean the control and purification of perverse tendencies. While it is true that the specific target is in fact not the object of erotic aggression, there are nevertheless real victims. There is physical or moral destruction in the event of childish or adult vandalism; other people are indirectly harmed if there is savage criticism of persons or things connected with the beloved; and the lover's own body or soul suffers if there is physical or moral masochism. At this stage of development perverse tendencies remain dangerous, because once they have been aroused, they are likely to set off a whole behavior pattern which, as we have shown above, consists of a mixture of stimulation and destruction.

Worried parents seeing their children persist in destructive behavior directed against their toys or themselves are well aware of this. They punish their children as soon as they see what is going on. And unless they are retarded, the children soon understand that they are doing something that is not considered right. Provided they are strong-minded enough to be able to take mental action to modify and control their perverse tendencies, they will spontaneously try to give up activities which call down adult disapproval on them, and which, in any event, they feel rather vaguely to be anarchical in character. It is only if they are incapable of such mental activity that perverse tendencies will persist until the children become adult, at which stage the greater force of erotic stimuli will intensify the perversions still further.

Perverse tendencies which are deflected from their specific targets onto displacement objects should properly be studied, as actual perversions are, by psychologists and criminologists, for in most cases there is actual destruction. We need not, therefore, spend time on them now. So far as our present study is concerned, only one thing need be noted about these forms of behavior, and this is that from their earliest youth, human beings have an astonishing capacity to substitute things, animate objects and individuals, for one another, quite indiscriminately. They are capable of substituting animals for humans, as in acts of bestiality; of using dolls in place of their mothers, whom they dare not try to trample underfoot; of replacing someone else's body by their own if this makes it easier to carry out erotic acts without fear of reprisals. This flexibility, which can also be seen in the animal world, is almost unlimited in human beings. Almost anything can represent something else, since the range of resemblances between them is nearly infinite. Of course, in real life the possibilities of substitution are not unlimited: a child cannot suck just any part of its body to console itself for the absence of its mother's breast. But human beings still have the resource of imagination, and once we reach the field of internal fantasies, reality and its limitations fall away, and the most superficial resemblances can give rise to unending chains of purely mental substitutions.

In saying that substitute perversions should be studied by psychopathologists, I do not mean that they never occur in normal people. If this were the case, how could we explain the interest normal people take in novels, films or plays whose leading characters give striking examples of displacement perversions? The spectacle of erotic pleasure in destruction or aggression leaves nobody unmoved, and arouses any latent perverse tendencies there may be in the beholder. Displacement perversions are of the greatest interest to normal people: they not only arouse curiosity, but, if they are artistically presented, provide intense pleasure. Furthermore, they do have a bearing on the fate of normal people, since they represent one possible course of development. Normal people can see, and indeed are bound to see, part of themselves reflected in perverts. It is only their strong-mindedness that has enabled them to escape not only from out-and-out perversions, but from displacement activities as well.

In normal human beings both perversions and displacement activities are inhibited. In this connection, I have already spoken on several occasions of mental powers, strong-mindedness and psychological development. The time has come to analyze these more subtle workings of the mind which enable people to avoid finding themselves in positions where they would have to act out on displacement targets the perverse tendencies aroused by the sight of an unattainable sexual object. Here we move into the field of the psyche itself. Hitherto, we have been dealing only with matters of instinct, such as the perception of simple erotic stimuli, the triggering of reactions that were a mixture of eroticism and aggressiveness, and the substitution of real displacement targets for the original object of desire. All these activities take place in the bodily organs at a strictly animal level. We are now going to see how, by a sort of transmutation, things of the body are replaced by things of the mind, and real instincts by fantasies, the purpose being to spare individuals the mishaps and risks of acting out perversions in the real world.

Human beings are endowed with imagination, and this faculty helps them to economize on real acts by replacing many of them by actions which only take place in the mind. When faced by the forces generated by perverse tendencies, it would be surprising if human beings did not have recourse to their imaginations, first to substitute imaginary behavior for real perversions and then to work on the imaginary acts in such a way as to eliminate the most aggressive, and hence the most dangerous, components.

Before describing the unconscious alchemy by which human beings try to remove the evil components of their imaginings, I shall have to explain how reality is transformed into imagination and perverse tendencies into corresponding imaginary perversions. In order to dispel any misunderstandings, I shall start by saying that it is not—as many psychoanalysts seem to believe—the energy generated by the instinctual tendencies that provides the driving power for the faculty of imagination. For this exists already, or at least it has an independent existence, although it is true that it is to some extent dependent upon the state of development reached by the brain. But once human beings achieve this power of imagination in the ordinary course of development, instinctive forces seize hold of it and use it both to avoid excessively dangerous real actions and to provide satisfactions that cannot be found in the real world. What gives the impression that these instinctive forces themselves create the faculty of imagination is the fact observed by psychopathologists that this faculty seems to be activated in the first instance by the urgent tasks facing the instinctive forces when they are unable to express themselves in real behavior. In other words, without a certain degree of tension, as might occur in an organism whose needs could all be expressed immediately in external actions, the faculty of imagination might never come into play, and would remain undeveloped. Clinical observation shows that one of the first uses of imagination both in children and in adults is to overcome instinctive perverse tendencies, not at the real level but in the mind.

III

UNCONSCIOUS SEXUALITY: INTERNAL CONFLICTS

Our task is becoming more difficult. As we come to examine mental attitudes the factors involved become not only more numerous but also more difficult to grasp. We have only to consider the astonishing capacity for displacement, camouflage and transformation displayed by the imagination. So far, to explain states of stimulation and inhibition, or tendencies to perversion, we had only to describe physiological reactions or visible behavior patterns. Reactions were easy to describe in terms of behavior. They were real events observable from the outside, not requiring any special use of language, and organized in a rigid pattern. Luckily for biologists, neither the properties of natural organisms nor the nature of the objects they affect are very often extensible. But when we tackle the human mind we enter an area of shifting sands where things are infinitely variable, where forms are fleeting and hardly susceptible to research. Moreover, there is one major disadvantage for the student: all his own emotions are involved. Any analysis of the mental side of sexuality is bound to end in self-analysis. This is the risk that was taken by the great pioneer Sigmund Freud, whose book *The Interpretation of Dreams* was really an analysis of himself, and since his time by all other psychoanalysts who have not shrunk from indirectly exposing themselves while writing about the laws governing the life of the mind.

Nowadays the risk is smaller for two reasons: First of all, either because of the progress in psychology or because times have changed, people are less ashamed than they were previously to reveal their inmost thoughts. Second, the mass of psychoanalytical discoveries is now sufficient to protect us against excessively subjective interpretations of people's inner worlds.

1

To start with, I would like to try to clear up the many misunderstandings about the nature of the *unconscious*. It is childish to consider it as a receptacle for fleeting ideas, most of them disagreeable, which must be carefully prevented from escaping. To take this attitude would be to accept the neurotic view of the unconscious adopted by obsessed or depressed individuals, who feel that their own personalities are like tanks filled chiefly with evil, or like a sort of digestive tract whose contents it would be indecent to discharge on the world at large. Very many of the nonprofessional criticisms on the subject of the unconscious arise from notions of this sort.

Some specialists in the study of mankind have rejected this notion and consider it absurd. But they see the unconscious as a part of the conscious and so ask, Why should not there be a part of this part—why not represent the life of the mind as an infinite series of ever smaller consciousnesses, one inside the other, just as the Renaissance biologists saw man as consisting of a whole series of little men, one inside the other?

Psychologists will have nothing to do with this sort of gulliverization of consciousness. Nor is it an inevitable outcome of the very notion of the unconscious, and it is a mistake to think that it is. To so believe is to accept a notion somewhat less childish than the nonprofessional criticism, but equally neurotic. We all know how attached some sick people become to their own shadows. It is as if they imagined such miniatures of themselves inside themselves—usually the organ with which their illness is associated. They identify their entire personalities with the affected organ and fondle it with a kind of narcissistic love. If this dissociation—this split between the total personality and a miniature personality, surrounded and nourished by the larger one—is applied to the unconscious mind instead of to an organ of the body, we have the theory of the unconscious which psychologists and philosophers so firmly reject.

The images associated with the idea of the unconscious are interesting because they show the unconscious at work interpreting mental activity in terms either of content and container or of internal objects, some of them excremental and some of them narcissistic. But precisely because they conform to the laws governing the workings of the unconscious, they cannot be used to define or describe it. For this, a more dynamic approach is needed. The unconscious is neither a receptacle nor an internal object. To start with, it implies the existence of mental activity prior to our thoughts and our conscious decisions. It is well known that people seeking the solution to a mathematical or technical problem continue to work on it in their sleep without knowing it. How much more likely it is that our unconscious is at work on the solution to vital emotional problems even when we are not completely awake or aware of the outside world.

We left the organism struggling with aggressive or forbidden sexual tendencies, which the imagination, or the power of representation, seizes on and starts to transform. But this mental activity is unconscious, and precedes any conscious thought. To put it in more physiological terms, we may say that finding the road to direct action barred, the chain reaction set up by erotic stimuli is diverted to the brain, where it works itself out in the imagination instead of in the real world. In psychological language, a more radical displacement occurs than that which we described in connection with perversions, in which the impulses are merely sidetracked from their specific targets. In this case, mental images are substituted for real objects in the external world. Perverse behavior patterns turn inward, so that real actions are replaced by fantasies.

It would be premature, however, to assume that all sexual behavior, taken in the broad sense, is thus transformed into mental activity. When tensions in the organism create desires that may not be fulfilled in the real world, the chain reaction is not shifted in its entirety into the field of the imagination. As the whole process has not yet been completed and release in sexual intercourse achieved, this cannot be represented by images in the unconscious.

Dreams are both incomplete and mysterious, and many people have therefore declared them to be unintelligible. It is indeed very rare for dreams to contain a complete act of sexual intercourse. Even when the dream ends in ejaculation or involuntary erection of the clitoris, the mental images are usually rather vague, more of an allusion than a detailed picture. Nonprofessionals are often surprised at how much can be discovered from their dreams, for they do not see their desires accurately reflected in these bits and pieces, as the expert does. Their scepticism is partly justified, especially when the interpretation is given in terms of behavior as precise and detailed as it would be in real life. It is well established that an incestuous dream does not contain a clear and precise picture of the sex act with a relative. To consider dreams in this way would be to put the cart before the horse and to interpret the vague beginnings of mental sex life in terms of clear-cut patterns that are not found until much later in the final stages of development.

To explain the enigmatic language of dreams, we need not immediately fall back on the theory of a censuring mechanism that filters out messages to make sure they are harmless. But we must understand that dreams occur at the point where body and mind meet. They also occur just at the moment when tendencies or impulses that have been prevented from developing freely turn into mental images, a point at which both the tendencies and the mental images are vague and undifferentiated. Dreams are not reproductions of conscious, waking mental activities. On the contrary, they lead to conscious thoughts in the same way as images foreshadow ideas or drafts foreshadow completed texts. They are the birthplace of a confused mixture of plans and ideas which the waking mind will have to prune and clarify, in order to bring them to fruition.

But while dreams are confused and irrational compared with the waking ideas that are built upon them, they are well organized compared with the notions they cause to develop in the imagination. It is here that we come back to the unconscious and its function, which is to internalize the impulses leading the individual toward a partner who is attractive and yet reluctant. The unconscious represents a form of mental activity whose laws are to be sought not in daily waking life but in the body's primary functions such as attack and seduction in their coarsest and most brutal form, i.e., pursuit, mutilation, consumption, incorporation, excretion and so on. The content of the unconscious is so rich and varied as to be discouraging; it can be understood only if we translate it into the most elementary terms, those of interrelated instinctual impulses whose synthesis forms the warp and woof of our unconscious and our waking dreams. The impulses themselves are like instinctive sequences of actions, borrowed from the behavior patterns connected with aggression and stimulation, and transferred, for the sake of internal equilibrium, into psychological or imaginary action. The unconscious is a genuine creation of the mind, produced by man's capacity to imagine, out of sequences of instinctive elementary actions which are grouped and linked together in accordance with an internal compulsion psychologists call the "pleasure principle."

I have described these elementary actions in the previous chapter. They are connected with what we have called perversions: that is, *aggressive actions* that may be subdivided into pursuit, conquest, mutilation and consumption; *acts of fear*, such as flight, retreat and concealment; or *erotic actions* that may be grouped under regurgitation, suckling, caressing and stimulating and soothing contacts. In the unconscious things take place just as if self-preservation and procreation were broken down into their primary components, thus yielding many broken series of actions that the human imagination rebuilds into a complete new whole in the mind.

In order to simplify the explanation, I have given concrete examples of instinctive sequences created in the mind. But it would be wrong to think that the unconscious consists of a set of working images of the sort that our conscious mind offers when we are awake. These conscious images are themselves a much-elaborated product of the unconscious, and the unconscious precedes both the pre-conscious and the conscious. And it is this that makes an explanation of the unconscious difficult. For how are we to describe something that exists in the mind, and that is both more than the perverse tendencies described in the previous chapter and less than the sets of images that occupy our waking consciousness? As a deliberate oversimplification it is fair to say that the unconscious is an autonomous structure composed of a series of instinctive tendencies and drives. The unconscious, which is both the starting point for all the fantasies of our mind and an emanation of the problems of our instinctive life, is itself a grouping of unfulfilled instinctive sequences. It is in fact an autonomous body of instincts grouped and structured in accordance with principles that I shall now discuss.

2

To recapitulate, when faced by his ambivalent tendencies toward aggression on the one hand and sexual activity on the other, an individual is responsible for preventing them from affecting any partner. He must even prevent them from being actually worked out on substitutes, whether outside objects or his own body. The only available solution is to replace all external objects by internal ones. And that is exactly what happens at the very beginning of unconscious mental existence. The individual withdraws into himself to play a complicated game that is both pseudo-sexual and pseudoaggressive. Instead of taking the form of real external behavior, the instincts related to aggression and seduction, flight and surrender, bring into being a relationship between the individual and some internal object he has substituted for a real external one. It is in this substitution that we find the basic mental mechanism of repression, which Freud called *Urverdrängung*.[1]

By giving the object of his impulses, and hence all the instinctive series of actions connected with it, a subjective existence, an individual achieves two separate effects. First, he makes the external object itself uninteresting from the standpoint of his erotic desires, so that it is desexualized or neutralized and ceases, at least for the time being, to have any erotic influence. And so, at the beginning of a love affair, after the initial excitement, a person may often be surprised to find that he is no longer interested in the partner by whom he was attracted and whom he had begun to love. When she is not present, he is upset to find that he cannot remember her face; when she is present, he is disturbed to find that he is bored. She is no longer the light of his eyes and cannot arouse him to either sympathy or antipathy. This is an example of desexualization or neutralization, which is a passing phase in the normal person, but a lasting one in a person with weak emotional attachments, who may suffer from it for many years or even throughout his life. But it is quite wrong to say that such people with schizophrenic tendencies are without emotions. When their inner lives are explored, they are discovered to have very intense passions indeed. The objects of these passions are, however, internal; for this reason real persons in the outer world cannot have any influence on them. Contact with the external world is cut off, for the whole internal network of communication is occupied by the many messages that are passing between the individual and purely internal objects.

When it is not permanent, this cessation of contact is only a small episode in the development of a sexual rela-

---

[1] R. Fliess' explanation, in his *Erogeneity and Libido* (New York, Schulte, 1956, pp. 41–44), is similar.

tionship; it usually occurs just after the first erotic attraction is felt. Faced by the danger of an explosion and the violent expression of instinctive reactions, the individual blows the fuse connecting him to the source of excitement. Only later, after patient unconscious processes in his own mind, and after violence has been transformed into tenderness, can contact be reestablished. At that time the relationship will benefit from an intense inner life that will give it a warmth and richness that would have been impossible without the temporary withdrawal.

The substitution of an internal object for a real person also divides the psyche into completely separate parts between which the instinctive sex actions can take place harmlessly and without regard to the real world. Withdrawal from the exciting but reluctant real partner goes hand in hand with the creation of a substitute mental object which has the same contradictory qualities, and so is just as exciting and yet as resistant as the real person it replaces. The mind thus loses its natural homogeneity and divides into separate nuclei, of which the first to appear is this internal object representing a two-sided reality.

At this point I feel it permissible to borrow the concept of *mitosis* from embryology and apply it to psychology. In speaking of a mitosis of the psyche, I am not merely making a comparison with the process that takes place in growth cells, but using the word in its most rigorous sense. Before it is called upon to provide a substitute object for instinctive behavior patterns, the psyche is only an undifferentiated capacity for image-making, a sort of unstructured elementary pseudopod of which all that is known is that its function will be to provide a substitute, in the form of mental behavior, when real behavior is forbidden or impossible. Once the initial external stimuli have been received, it becomes necessary to provide instinctive behavior with an outlet that has no impact on the outside world, and at this point there emerges from the undifferentiated mass a nucleus with properties similar to those of any real person who might take pleasure in simultaneously exciting and rejecting the individual in question.

As we are talking psychology, we ought to base this abstract description of mitosis of the psyche on specific subjective phenomena. This presents no problem; we have only to think of the emotional upset nearly everyone experiences when they first begin to have sexual emotions. They feel as if their whole personality were being changed and reorganized around a different focal point, or as if it were no longer a conflict-free homogeneous substance but contained a growing foreign body that was likely to be a source of tension and conflict.

We have not yet reached the point at which the individual's conscious thought is entirely taken up by a loved one. There are a number of stages before then. At this point, there is no specific object on the horizon. As a matter of fact, at this point the individual repulses anybody who offers, feeling that the drama must first be played out in his soul with something inside him that is not all of him. He would be unable to put a name on this thing he feels living inside him, which organizes his instinctive forces in a new way. Indeed he refuses to do so, rejecting all the names offered him and saying that there is nobody. If it were possible to name this something, it would become too real and so defeat its initial purpose, which is to isolate him from all the real people smothering him with their aims and their contradictory messages. This something which is nothing—neither father nor mother, God nor devil, prince nor princess, master nor mistress—can turn into any of these as the psyche develops toward consciousness sometime in the future. But in the beginning it is undifferentiated, a thing both external and internal, an unnamed but real object that is both stimulating and paralyzing. As ambiguous as all the real beings it replaces and enfolds, it is both aggressive and erotic; it is a compound of anonymous fellow beings; it is a sort of generalized "Someone" created by the psyche, and its function is to represent and replace all the human beings in the hard outer world.

One of the main elements in the feeling of confusion at the start of sexual life is this sense of internal disorganization that accompanies the creation of the nameless but attractive and frightening thing which modern psychologists call the internal object, and which it is perhaps legitimate to compare with the "Sacred Thing" whose ambivalent nature Rudolf Otto has described so well.

With the creation of this internal object and the appearance in the psyche of this nucleus uniting so many contradictory qualities that it is a sort of crystallization of seduction-rejection behavior, an individual can do without other people. But the price is high. For this development implants in the mind once and for all a sense of contradiction. As long as the individual takes some notice of the real world, meaning the people around him, he adapts to their moods, reacting to kindness and affection by responses denoting attachment and a lowering of defenses, and to hostility, by withdrawal or combativeness. As his friends' behavior varied over a period of time, his own attitudes could be adjusted and his moods fitted to the same rhythm. But if he now develops in his own psyche an object that can ignore the variations taking place in the real world, he is faced by something that is at one and the same time—and not successively—good-tempered and bad-tempered, like Janus inviting mankind simultaneously to make peace and war. The normal succession of well-wishing and evil-wishing that takes place in the real world is thus replaced by a sort of contradictory coexistence in the internal something, and its effect is to make the individual a permanent prey to the conflict between love and hostility, sexual relaxation and aggressive tension. What is rhythmic in the outside world becomes discordant in the mind.

3

And so at the very moment when sexual needs begin to increase there is a very painful internal dissociation. Concupiscence increases and so does irascibility, to use philosophical terms. Pleasure as such, irrespective of any specific mate, becomes extraordinarily attractive. At the same time, the person affected becomes more bad-tempered still. As he does not immediately obtain the expected pleasure—which is floating about in an unreal world—he becomes irritated over trifles. The vagueness of the causes of bad temper and desire make both these characteristics seem like absolutes, existing in their own right independently of the real people they affect. Psychologists have certainly been right in saying that the life of the psyche flows from a group of autonomous impulses which in the beginning are not related to any specific person.

It is impossible to construct a theory of human relations without examining impulses as such, that is, as forces independent of any real objects. But it would be wrong to assume that the psychology of human relations is no more than a study of such impulses. For in their pure state they represent only a stage in the development of the psyche—a stage in which instinctive actions, disassociated from any biological reality, operate for themselves alone, thus acquiring a completely autonomous existence and becoming a source of pure drive.

In the animal world there is only sexual behavior, either purely aggressive or a mixture of aggression and eroticism. Among animals, everything takes place in the real world;

and such terms as "tendencies," "latent impulses" and "pure drives" have, therefore, little meaning. The misuse of terms arises from making analogies with the behavior of humans, the only creatures in the animal world in whom instinctive sex urges, aggression, and combinations of the two develop internally, to become something separate and autonomous called *appetitus concupiscibilis et irascibilis* by the medieval scholastics, "passions" by Descartes and "impulses" by modern psychologists (Triebe). It would be a major error to see behind these concepts elemental instincts common to animals and human beings alike; they refer only to something created by the unconscious workings of the human mind. This something is a sort of formalized system of the instinctive urges which in the animal world lead to sexual behavior, whether entirely aggressive or partly benign in character, but in human beings become separate, unreal and autonomous because of the mechanism of repression.

There is one phenomenon which is so common that it causes no comment and yet is an excellent example of the autonomous nature of these impulses. If a man is deprived of sexual relations and is shut up alone in his room, a whole host of erotic ideas and images will invade his mind. He starts dreaming of lascivious women, whom he has never met or who are composed of many different women. He imagines committing acts that are sometimes tender and sometimes cruel. But if this man is asked what woman he has in mind he will be unable to answer. Often, indeed, he will deny that his imaginings have anything to do with the beautiful and virtuous woman he is actually courting. If he is asked whether he experiences physical excitement at the sight of women in the real world he will often say "No." What is remarkable here is the difference between the wealth of images that can be thought up by a solitary dreamer and the poverty of his reactions in the real world.

In the animal world things are very different. Animals' erotic reactions certainly depend on the state of their hormones, but the presence of some external stimulus is absolutely necessary. Animals seldom display erotic reactions when no stimulus is present, and the main effect of the physiological state is to cause them actively to seek a mate. In human beings, on the contrary, things are the other way around. It is when a man has no specific partner that the cycle of erotic reactions begins; when the person who causes the excitement is present all trigger mechanisms are blocked. This reversal of the biological situation found in nature is a good illustration of the autonomous nature of human impulses. Man has a system of instinctive reactions which remain latent as long as the many stimuli available in real life keep him distracted, but which come to life to produce a mass of images and ideas once the tumult of the outer world is stilled.

It may be said that this example is pathological. This is perfectly true if it is agreed that by "pathological" all we mean is the exaggeration of a normal state or the halting of development at some intermediate stage.

In all human beings whose development is not arrested at the level of mere sexual reaction there grows up an autonomous system of aggressive sexual impulses quite independent of real life. Under the continuous contradictory stimulus of the internal object, the instinctive reactions cease to be temporary and adapted to external circumstances and become permanently fixed and independent of the contingencies of real life. This is how there develops, in a psyche that starts by being quite undifferentiated, a nucleus that I shall call the "impulse nucleus," a sort of permanent instrument at the service of aggressive or erotic reactions. With the appearance of this new nucleus, which marks the second stage in the mitosis of the psyche, contradiction becomes a permanent factor in the individual's life.

Once again I would like to stress the contrast between animals and human beings. In a state of nature, where the behavior of things and fellow creatures is straightforward —either frankly sexual or frankly aggressive—contradiction presents no problem. Animals' reactions are either aggressive or sexual, depending on circumstances, and only both together for a very short time at the beginning of stimulation. But, even then, this hybrid reaction, part aggressiveness and part sexual desire, lasts only as long as the stimulus itself is ambiguous. As soon as the stimulus is gone or stops being ambiguous, the internal contradiction disappears. Human beings, however, experience states of contradiction quite independent of the sympathetic or antipathetic attitudes of the people around them. These are internal and fairly long-lasting contradictions between sexual desire and aggression, between erotic reactions and flight or attack. What is specifically human in this is the existence at one and the same time of the two opposing tendencies—sexual desire and aggression—without reference to changes in people with whom the individual is in contact.

The thoughts of impotent neurotics are often split between contradictory fantasies, whose simultaneous existence is extremely painful. When they imagine themselves caressing a consenting woman, they are also clawing and wounding her. They cover her body with poisoned kisses and stimulate her most sensitive parts with red-hot irons. In speaking of such morbid and sadistic imaginings we cannot even say that gentleness gradually turns into cruelty or vice versa, for the two occur simultaneously. While it is difficult to imagine this dualism in real life, in the world of fantasy it is quite possible. It is in a sense a single instinctive impulse loaded with both tenderness and cruelty. It is only because of the limitations of analytical thinking that contradictory images seem to follow one another; at the level of the unconscious they actually occur as two aspects of a single reaction.

Once we accept that the internal object is something both stimulating and recalcitrant, it is easy to understand the dual nature of the impulse nucleus, which Freud explained by his theory of the dual nature of instincts. On the one hand is the instinct toward life, or *libido,* on the other the instinct toward death or aggression, or—according to psychoanalysts who like their symmetry—*destrudo.* In our own terminology we would say that an individual's impulse nucleus, awakened and intensified by the two-sided internal object, divides into two parts, each a response to one side of the internal object. Unfortunately, however, this description is rather misleading. The two-sided impulse nucleus does not reflect either separate instincts or distinct and discontinuous elements. Furthermore, far from occurring at the start of the process of unconscious transmutation, the clear-cut separation between vitalizing sexuality and destructive aggression comes about later, precisely as the result of this process. For, only after a sustained and serious effort of internal analysis can an individual separate the aggressive factors from the erotic ones. In the early period of the development of the psyche there is only a single instinctive reaction which contains both elements. Contemporary psychologists speak of a fusion of the two instincts, as if they started by existing separately and were then woven together in a sort of mental braid. In fact the reverse is true: the sex instinct and the aggressive instinct are the products of mental analysis. In the original impulse nucleus there are only mixed components; these are later separated out into two homogeneous elements: the sex impulse and the aggressive impulse.

The view of the impulse nucleus as separated into two distinct components arises from another characteristic of the human mind: the temptation to explain any phenomenon by subsequent events. We shall only escape this error by resorting to the data already available, that is, that the internal object has two faces and that the impulse nucleus is a response to their contradictory pulls. Once we accept this, the contradictory nature of the impulse nucleus can be explained by analogy: the instinctive reactions arising from the impulse nucleus and not yet defined are merely urges that could be part of either a purely erotic behavior pattern or a purely destructive one. The impulse nucleus is seeking both pleasure and destruction, because it is as yet committed to neither of these. The instinctive reactions it contains are still too undifferentiated, like atoms which may be used either for peace or for war.

The instinctive urge, for example, to lay hands on someone may be embodied both in the action of caressing and the action of hitting out. The content of the impulse nucleus is only a collection of urges of this sort, so undifferentiated that they can serve either positive or negative motives. It is the lasting hesitation in choosing between the two possible courses of action that makes people suffer from a sense of contradiction once the two-sided internal object has been created inside them and they have withdrawn within themselves all their instinctive drives toward natural sexual relations and aggressiveness.

4

There is another contradiction—that between duty and instinct, renunciation and spontaneity—which is even harder to bear.

What is rather surprising, and therefore worthy of attention, is the fact that the human conscience does not begin by objecting to immoral acts in the real world. Psychopaths—people whose reactions follow one another at an unusually rapid pace, so that the time between stimulation and consummation of any act is very short—are not smothered by scruples. Even in more complex individuals, like certain homosexuals who are easily led into perverse acts, the feeling of guilt applies less to the perverse acts themselves than to intimate thoughts and desires that are really quite harmless because they are quite unreal. Most ordinary people are surprised by the fact that many criminals seem to feel no remorse. If the average man knew more about criminals' hidden feelings, he would be even more astonished by the contrast between the delicacy of their scruples over some harmless aspect of their inner life and their lack of concern about the real crimes they commit. This contrast is certainly illogical and an incontestable sign of immaturity, but it is completely in keeping with elementary expressions of guilt. One characteristic of the mature adult is that he knows when remorse is important; he can appreciate his faults for what they are and can pass judgment on his real acts. Since this is an ideal attained by human beings only at the age of maturity and experience, and even then often incompletely, it is reasonable to conclude that it is not a natural phenomenon at the beginning of the life of the mind.

Dramas of conscience start by being enacted entirely within the individual. Is there any remorse more bitter than that which is felt following certain dreams, or in connection with imaginary desires and situations? How much more moral mankind would be if humans felt the same anguish about their real acts as they feel about their sinful thoughts! Moral education consists entirely of shifting guilt and its accompanying sensations from the realm of fantasy to the real world. But the fact that a shift of this sort is necessary throws light on the unconscious, which is the point where notions of guilt first appear.

The first crises of human conscience are played out in

the imagination, not in the real world. They are not concerned with preventing the repetition of forbidden or blameworthy actions, but with preventing the development of impulses which may never have given rise to any actual behavior. A loose woman suffers less remorse than a spinster fighting her fantasies; the latter is never free from the pressure of impulses which are usually violent precisely because they are never satisfied. The loose woman, on the contrary, is aware only of the problems of reality; untroubled by the problems that arise from interiorization, she can lead a fickle and dangerous existence, her spirit free from internal monsters. Once her system of sexual reactions is set in motion, she moves through the various opportunities life offers to frequent fulfillment in sex acts. The internal object, the ambivalent impulse nucleus, the inhibitions controlling this nucleus, all the things underlying the life of the unconscious, play only a minor part and have little effect on the spontaneous character of her routines of attack and seduction. As she has no internal hesitations, she behaves with complete abandon, and this is her trump card in dealing with men who dislike being as complex as they are and would like to return to a state of nature. It also excites the unconscious jealousy of the so-called respectable woman, who is paralyzed by the system of taboos that control her mind.

But such a woman would of course be wrong to try to return to a less complex condition. For the development of the mind is irreversible: the proper solution to such conflict lies beyond the unconscious, in an easy, gracious expression of the contents of the deepest levels of the mind, and in a positive use of all the secret aspects of psychic life, for the purpose of drawing nearer to others. Once these conflicts are overcome, the personality will become richer, fuller and deeper; but I am not going to describe this development yet. We must progress step by step and must begin by understanding the nature of the intimate taboos. We have just seen that they are not at first directed to real behavior but to images of behavior, not to real actions in the outside world but to possible courses of action springing from the part of the mind that I have called the impulse nucleus.

We know that this nucleus is permanently activated by the two-sided internal object. It is a nest of contradictions, and the individual will not benefit in the least from having it grow larger in its original form. The greater the attention paid to the internal object, the bigger this instrument of aggressive and sexual impulses will grow. It can indeed become monstrous, and this means that the feeling of contradiction will also become intolerably intense. Now, it is certainly to prevent the excessive growth of this perverse state of contradiction that the psyche develops another nucleus, whose function is to limit and reduce the power of the internal object and to prevent existence from being cluttered up by the contradictions inherent in a life governed by instinct alone.

At this point it is worth repeating that the drama I have been describing takes place on a strictly private internal stage, far removed from reality. There is no question of inhibiting real actions or impeding real behavior. If this is so, how are we to understand the reducing function of the new nucleus? How can we conduct a struggle against something which is going on inside, a purely formal working of the mind, in fact what I have called the formalized system of sexual and aggressive impulses? We can do so only if we deliberately bring that system into disrepute.

We must beware of considering any action by this Superego (Freud's term for this second nucleus) as a real activity opposing other real activities. Notions of this kind are always being put forward; they arise from our inability to understand the special nature of psychic phenomena. These

are not simply miniature activities. The reducing function
I have described in connection with the new nucleus does
not show itself in an actual move in the opposite direction.
Just as a person's psychic tendencies are nonmaterial, so are
the defenses he invents in order to avoid falling victim to
the contradictions inherent in the tendencies themselves.
We are therefore concerned not with action but with eval-
uation, not with an actual flight from these tendencies but
with a judgment regarding the undesirable nature of the
tendencies, not with a force of repression but with a judicial court. The second nucleus, whose purpose is to assure
internal equilibrium, is the organ of formal prohibition.

The Superego is a sort of legislative and judicial agency,
a spontaneous creation of the psyche, which assumes the
right of absolute control over the whole system of internal
desires or impulses. It keeps some and throws out others. It
is a more or less absolute monarch. The more confused and
disordered the desires, the more likely is it to be all-power-
ful. It is easy to govern a people whose intentions are either
frankly benevolent or frankly hostile. But the exercise of
power becomes difficult when the populace consists of
groups whose avowed aims do not coincide with their hidden goals. The result is a vicious circle: the more underground parties there are, the tougher the ruling power becomes. But the tougher the ruling power becomes, the
greater the number of elusive underground groups that are
formed. This is what goes on in the mind when sexual desires are an inextricable confusion of goodwill and hostility.
The Superego has great difficulty in separating the good
from the bad and tries to do away with the whole lot in
order to have some peace and quiet. But the desires conceal themselves still more skillfully in self-defense against
this blind exercise of authority, thus provoking the internal judge to still greater vigilance. This explains why the
first stirrings of sex life are marked by impulses that be-

come stronger and more urgent as the adverse judgment is harsher and less discriminating. Similarly the sense of guilt will be more agonizing as the desires are driven further underground.

We all carry about within us a judge whose harshness varies from person to person. If he is too severe and lacking in discernment, the desires rebel and become simultaneously frightening and fascinating, so that they are difficult to control and organize. If he is reasonable, the desires are viewed with goodwill even if they are not really approved of. As their existence is tolerated within certain limits, they reveal themselves without too much trouble and agree to play a normal part in the psychological life of the individual.

These metaphors based on the notion of an internal judge of varying severity have a genuine grounding in the real life of the mind. In response to the formation of the impulse nucleus—the organ of aggression and sexual desires—the psyche develops within itself the inhibiting nucleus, an opposing organ whose function is to call a halt whenever the impulses seem to be getting out of hand.

These two nuclei are on terms of friendship or antagonism, obedience or revolt, goodwill or hostility, just as are, in the social community, law and human needs, governors and governed.

In all normal human development, there is a dissociation between these two nuclei—the moral side, with its legislative and judicial functions, and the impulse side, which shows itself in a set of gross desires—and the two parts of the psyche live together on terms of more or less goodwill. Some people judge their desires with great severity; others, while not approving of them all, view them with an indulgent eye, which is a sign not of weakness but of serene strength.

But let us for the moment leave aside the question of differences between individuals, and in retracing the various stages of psychic development and progress toward the capacity for a satisfying sexual relationship, investigate the ways in which the internal judge prevents desire from becoming excessive. This judge is not a force opposing other forces, since the desires, a formalized system of instinctive reactions, have no real energy of their own. The function of the new psychic tribunal is to act as judge: it punishes, forbids, permits, approves and rewards. Traditional morality makes good sense in speaking of the "voice of conscience." Clinical observation shows that it is more like a voice than a force—a voice that administers justice and lays down the law.

But in whose name? It cannot function in its own name, as this would deprive its judgments of any significance. It must do so in the name of an objective, impersonal authority. All constitutions governing human society, and the punishments for contravening them, are proclaimed in the name of a king or a republic. The same thing applies in the psychic world: the voice of conscience speaks in someone's name. And so a new internal object with the voice of authority or law is created to support and justify the actions of the new tribunal, and it is in its name that prohibitions, bans and punishments are handed down.

The castration complex, which I have already described and which seems to have some effect on every man and woman, even if there is no real threat from parents or other adults, is strengthened by the new internal object. In order to suppress all sexual activities (which, at this stage, are necessarily perverse), the mind seems to raise the horrid specter of a being capable of destroying or damaging the sex organs. Psychoanalysts currently believe that the castration complex is no more than the metaphorical means by which the internal judge achieves its goal: the suppression of all instinctive sexual reactions. Even though it has no reality, it is nonetheless intensely felt in the most primitive part of the psyche.

This internal object—which is the source of prohibitions and punishments—can take on many forms. In itself it is as anonymous, amorphous and undifferentiated as the first internal object. It is the basic source of all our conscious or preconscious representations of prohibitions. It is, as it were, the quintessential ban. It is only through the action of the imagination that the ban takes on specific forms: a monster likely to injure us, a father or mother to punish us, a loyal person to despise us, or a God to condemn us to death or send us to hell. By means of the data collected by perception and thought, the psyche gives the internal ban an objective form, which it then projects on the screen of our consciousness.

The well-known Oedipus complex is one of the forms projected in this way. It is probably universal, not in the sense that it is found in every civilization, but in the sense that any major work of art is universal. The complex can be understood by anybody, and it is one of the most accurate reflections of man's anxieties about his sexual activities. If we say that someone's sex life is paralyzed by Oedipus factors, we mean that he regards all sex acts as an incestuous relationship with his mother and hence likely to be punished by his father. The result of this complex is naturally to strengthen any inhibitions the person may have. In the story of Oedipus, the original internal object is represented by the mother, the secondary internal object by the father, who is dead but still present to enforce the ban. Our dreams are constructions, on the same model as Sophocles' play. Like the play, and most other works of art, they arise from the fact that within the psyche sexual desires laden with aggressive overtones encounter the attraction of an irresistible internal object and, simultaneously, the horrors of a fundamental ban.

If we turn to consider the method of operation of the Superego, we shall find that it is like a prompt but violent judge, more like a hangman than a sage. In a word, it threatens. It is like a muted voice which in the early stages is heard only indistinctly, stirring thoughts of vague but terrible dangers on the path to sexual fulfillment. Then, as perception and imagination develop, the threats become clearer and stronger because they even seem quite reasonable.

An individual tempted to indulge in sexual activities may become afraid of being thrown into hell and enduring eternal torment, of being spurned by father and mother, his vital forces being lost and himself becoming mad or ill. In T.B. sanatoria, cases are often found in which the patient believes that the damage to his lungs was caused by supposed sexual excesses. And many young people attribute the weakening of memory to the satisfaction of some new sexual desire. There are even some adults for whom every act of intercourse is a step toward death. Basing themselves on the example of a few old men with heart conditions who have in fact died while having intercourse, they measure out their sex acts with care and on each occasion fear some fatal damage to their mental or physical health. The power of the imagination to lead people into error is really astonishing, if we consider that the life-giving act itself is turned by the imagination into a risk of death. All the age-old stories about the praying mantis, bees and other species whose unfortunate males meet their death at the moment of the act of love are naturally quoted in support of this mistaken view.

Nevertheless it would be wrong to consider the role of the secondary internal object and its bans as entirely negative. For while it prohibits, it also authorizes certain acts. It distinguishes good from evil. It may be excessively harsh and tyrannical in the early stages of sex life, but this is because of the confused nature of sex drives at that time. They are both good and bad; they contain goodwill mixed with hostility and even cruelty. More correctly, they are undifferentiated instinctive urges which may equally well be used for love or hate. And so internal authority starts by decreeing a complete ban in order to make sure that everything tainted with hostility or aggression is first eliminated. In order to get rid of the weeds, the whole crop is cut down. But little by little, authority begins to take a more sophisticated view and to develop a new discernment. Less sweeping in its convictions, it becomes better able to distinguish between good and evil in the autonomous instinctive urges. At first, the distinctions it makes are cursory and superficial, but as time goes on it succeeds in analyzing the components of the instinctive urges and separating the acceptable ones from those that are harmful to the individual. But if there is to be any appreciation of the exact worth of these urges, it is clear that they must express themselves in some way that enables the authority to make a judgment.

Before going on to analyze the progress toward arriving at an internal distinction between good and bad, between what is approved and what is not insofar as sex life is concerned, I would like to issue a warning against considering this progress in terms of clear-cut conscience, as if the individuals we are talking about had already reached the stage of being able to identify accurately most of the instinctive urges beginning to take shape within them. We have not got so far; we are still in the stage where nothing has either a name or an image. Indeed it might be well to ask what has been achieved by what I have called the mitosis of the psyche, i.e., the spontaneous differentiation of the psyche into separate nuclei or organs.

We are now in a position to describe the anatomy and the physiology of the human psyche, and we must say that the two together make up what psychoanalysts call the unconscious. At the lower level, there is the impulse nucleus, the organ generating tendencies containing a mixture of sexual tenderness and aggression which reacts to an internal object that is both attractive and heartbreakingly reluctant. Above, we have seen how an inhibiting organ or defense mechanism called the Superego reacts to anything connected with law or prohibitions. Between the two nuclei, there are frequent but rather strained relations. This is of course the same state of affairs we have observed in connection with the purely physiological reactions: the sympathetic and parasympathetic systems, the stimulatory and inhibitory hormones, and the "go" and "stop" nerve centers. The psychological system is a copy of the physiological system at a higher level. The opposition between impulse and prohibition, and between pleasure and the law, follows the same pattern.

But I do not wish to carry the comparison any further. The most important thing to remember is that the nuclei we have discovered are both dynamic and purely abstract. Although we have had to make use of metaphors from waking life to explain them, the opposing tendencies so far described have no definite form. They are pure drives, a desire for pleasure and an inclination toward repression. Nothing has yet been given a name or an image. The segments of sexual pleasure exist in themselves; they are directed toward an internal object which is of course not a real thing but something soon to be built up from bits and pieces of real persons. Similarly, the movements toward inhibition and rejection exist in the pure state; they are activated by another internal object, which will later take the form of a castrating father, a cruel god or a pitiless law, without ever coinciding exactly with any real agency of authority in human society. It is a nameless, imageless conflict, a deep and lasting split, without which human beings would not be what they are. And its infinitely varied manifestations are to be found in the legends, myths and religions of the world.

5

The unconscious, a collection of pure timeless drives, develops only bit by bit. As people are subject to the pressure of contradictory desires and torn between pleasure and duty, their imaginations spontaneously produce fictional situations on which they can freely practice finding solutions without any of the risks inherent in real action. To put it in a metaphor which may be of some help, it is as if when asked whether aggressive sexual tendencies were permissible or legal, the inner authority replied that it cannot give an answer in the abstract and must see all the documentation, and the person then invented a number of stories and asked the authority to identify the good and evil in them. To grasp the actual mechanism we must have a clear idea of the part played by the imagination, the faculty that allows people to prepare for action by providing fictitious models of behavior in advance. At this stage, I shall point only to the intolerable situation of people struggling with contradictory internal objects: in trying to find some solution to their problems they invent fictional circumstances and activities. Many psychiatrists believe that the raving inventions of psychotics are the result of a spontaneous attempt at self-cure, and are an arrangement on an imaginary stage of the many aspects of genuine internal conflicts. Can we not say the same of human dreams, which may be described as the raving inventions of normal people?

Such dreams are not openly concerned with sex. They consist of complicated stories, and the problems are raised delicately and indirectly without seeming to be mentioned.

The instinctive aggressive sex drives are wrapped up in unlikely tales, which are nevertheless the first attempts at statements on which judgments are required. Moreover, these judgments are given in the pictorial language used by children and primitives, for example: "Woman is a bottomless pit in which we can only go on falling forever; however beautiful she may be, you must still beware of her, because she is really a witch; watch out for mortal blows and for injury from the knives, hammers or cars of your chief rivals, etc." As they are images from the unconscious, dreams tell both of impulses and of the defenses against them.

People are often afraid of their dreams. They are prepared to accept them only when they are thoroughly filtered and matured. Generally speaking, it is only the greatest artists who dare accept their dreams in their original crude form, offering frightening and extreme pleasures and punishments. Such people are masters of sounds, colors, images, words and ideas through which they can allow their unconscious to come to the surface in all its terrifying forms without fearing its fascination. At the other end of the scale, there is no doubt that some people become perverts or criminals for lack of inoffensive means of expressing themselves. Their actions are the only ways they can express and purify themselves.

It would be wrong to think that the dreams of perverts and artists are more sadistic or masochistic than those of ordinary people. Otherwise, why should ordinary people so much enjoy reading books of violence or sensational newspapers? In their original form, everybody's dreams are violent. Only after a long process of filtration and purification do they become harmless or amusing. Children's earliest dreams are usually nightmares, and it takes a long time before they are replaced by more agreeable ones.

The first images to occur in the unconscious are inevitably violent. We have only to think of the nature of the impulses demanding action and the primary defenses that are put up against them. In doing so we should bear in mind the nature of the urges that have been "internalized," that is, withdrawn from real life. They are concerned with incorporation, excretion, rape—in brief, violent and brutal sexuality. Expressed as images and suggestive tales, these urges turn into sadistic or masochistic stories whose characters, all versions of the dreamer himself, attack or wound others, are felled, or fall under a car or over a precipice, cry or console others. If to these symbolic representations of perversions we add the forms taken by the prohibitory Superego, the appearance of severe, authoritarian and even armed characters in dreams is easy to understand.

Early dreams do not usually allow sex acts to appear in the agreeable form in which they occur in real life. Such dreams indeed develop only fairly late in human life, after a long period in which the images of violence and filth that by unconscious sexuality produces as its representation of pleasure have been filtered out. Let us go one step further and ask whether a human being ever reaches the degree of innocence where sexual union, the extreme and ecstatic expression of the love of two bodies for one another, is ever quite free of the taint of something brutal, sordid and criminal. Human nature is such that even the heights of physical love are sullied by hateful images. And because it is like this, the social bans, which are easily borne by anyone enjoying a satisfactory sex life, never completely lose the overly severe features which they have in our unconscious life. Temptations and prohibitions, the two poles of psychic tension, together produce the kaleidoscopic images that populate our dreams and give them the violent content which is the source of all great works of imagination.

The reader may be surprised that I have so far made no distinction between men and women. This is because all the stages of development from initial inhibition up to and including the formation of the unconscious (impulses, prohibitions and contradictions between the two nuclei) are almost identical in the two sexes. In both of them, erotic excitement turns into a perverse impulse, a mixture of aggression and sexuality. Furthermore, in both sexes the perverse impulse is internalized and directed to an internal object. Finally, a prohibitory object develops in opposition to the impulse nucleus in both males and females. In short, the unconscious is not only timeless, in the view of most psychoanalysts, but also sexless.

Differences between the sexes, particularly anatomical differences, begin to play an important part only at the stage where the unconscious takes shape, and in the preconscious organization of dreams. Of course, it is not the sex organs themselves, whether penis or vagina, that immediately start haunting the dreams of men and women. Their tendencies have not yet developed far enough to allow them to think of these organs quite so openly. In fact the opposite occurs. The unconscious starts by using the most visible and obvious anatomical differences in making up its stories and dreams. Thus, two sorts of imaginary creatures appear: the ones armed, strong and combative; the others unarmed, weak and destined to be victims or martyrs. It is this generalized image of men and women that gives significance to the details. On the one hand, if the role allotted by the unconscious to the male requires strength and action, it is fairly certain that the penis, the seat of male sexuality, will be represented by a dangerous weapon; and this is indeed an image that recurs very frequently in dirty jokes throughout history. On the other hand, if the aggressive role in these internal dramas is allotted to the female, at some point the vagina will certainly become a horrible cave in which there is every likelihood of being wounded and bled dry before being finally swallowed up and never seen again.

It is frightening to think that many people spend their whole lives seeing both individuals of the opposite sex and themselves through the magnified and distorted image of men and women created by their unconscious. Of course, any woman in real life is likely to react at times with a certain amount of aggressiveness. This is unimportant unless it awakes in us the latent image of the consuming monster or the horrid cave. If it does, however harmless the reaction may actually have been, it will induce a state of panic out of all proportion to the actual importance of the external stimulus, but corresponding to the terrifying size of our internal image. I say without any hesitation that most high-strung, irritable people carry about within them a great many terrifying images of this sort, through which they interpret the minor events of everyday life. Think of all the women who interpret the least sign of authority in their spouse as an indication of a tendency toward tyranny and egotism, this tendency being of course a figment of their imaginations.

Powerful dichotomies of the forms attacker-victim, attacked-attacker, attacker-attacked are bound to appear in the minds of people with perverse tendencies and aggressive sexuality. They are then projected onto real people and events, which thus become huge and terrifying, commensurate with the size of the images created by the imagination. The more intense the latent aggression with which sexuality is charged, the more persistent are these fictional magnifications likely to be. It is only cultural chance that determines whether the dichotomies are projected onto ethnic groups—Greeks and barbarians, Jews and Gentiles, plainsmen and mountaineers—or onto different sexual groups, meaning men and women. But it is worth noting that wherever the tragic beam of opposition alights, the imaginary foe (barbarian, pagan or member of the opposite sex) exercises a great attraction. Intense fear is mixed with an equally intense attraction, to which individuals considered particularly powerful or capable do not respond as ordinary mortals do. The explanation of this fascination is to be found in the nature of perverse sexuality. The aggressive component of the sexual urge is attributed to the object of the erotic excitement, who thus becomes a fantastic being—at one and the same time terribly dangerous and the bearer of unknown pleasures. The duality of the sexual instinct and the internal object is applied to external realities which are far enough apart and far enough away to lend themselves to all sorts of falsifications.

Another remarkable thing is the ease with which an individual's preconscious may ignore his true sexual anatomy altogether. If a man considers Woman as the incarnation of a force that will always win in the end, he will really think that he is a woman and deny that he has a penis, or turn it into a sort of breast to be sucked by his mate. If a woman regrets that she is the weaker partner and is jealous of her man's superior position, she will seek on her body or inside it anything that can symbolize virility: hair, breast, legs, brain or child. Reality is treated with scant respect by the imagination, which takes from it any details it likes and uses them to produce plays composed by the unconscious. Dreams are not to be explained by the objective properties of the real world, but by the argument that goes on in the unconscious, which is itself composed, first, of aggression and sexuality, and second, of the opposing forces of pleasure and prohibition. The characters taking part in dreams—men and women, old people and young people, monsters and benefactors, friends and enemies—are only symbols in a script. And what is the script about? It represents the argument that goes on inside anyone trying to sort out the contradictions of his unconscious in order to separate sexuality from aggression and reconcile pleasure with prohibition. However tragic they may be, neuroses and psychoses have something in common with dreams, as they are themselves dreams which, though they may trespass too far on reality, do represent a genuinely creative activity and an attempt to overcome the dilemmas of perversion.

Springing as they do from the depths of the mind, the earliest dreams of individuals, as of humanity as a whole, are by and large tragic. They deal with blood, theft, rape, torture, horrible or comic transformations, life and death. Men and women are strongly contrasted. Sometimes it is the male, sometimes the female who has the dominant role and is the perfect being. The two sexes pass in turn from glory to destruction, from victory to defeat. In fact, dreams provide a violent saga of the imaginary struggle between the sexes, and the real conflict is not a quarter as fierce.

At this point many readers will refuse to follow me, as they refuse to accept many psychoanalysts' statements when they are thrown off point-blank without some qualification. They will find the picture too black. They will say that they themselves simply do not suffer from the perverted images, the sadistic or masochistic pleasures, the wild and childish fears that I have described. But they will certainly admit that they understand what I am talking about, and that is enough for my purposes; for this alone proves that some deeply hidden residue of the aggressive and perverse tendencies of the unconscious still persists within them. The truth is that we soon forget the crises from which we emerge victorious, and that the tensions of the unconscious reach our consciousness only in a very weakened form.

The early violent dreams are a way of draining off latent aggression and perversions. For we do not necessarily have to perform in real life the acts we accomplish in dreams.

This is one of the great benefits of the imagination, which substitutes imaginary actions projected onto the internal screen for acts that would be fatal if carried out in real life. The very act of dreaming is in itself a sort of purification. The basic components of the unconscious (perverse temptations and cruel prohibitions) continue to invade the life of the mind, but in a much-refined form that gradually becomes more acceptable. Many people think that it is dangerous to express their hidden desires, but they are confusing expression with achievement. In truth, human beings suffer far less from failure to achieve something than from an inability to express themselves, and this is known to every psychoanalyst who has watched his patients trying to make themselves understood. Such patients often blame the world for not bringing them in contact with people patient enough to help them express themselves, in other words to relieve themselves by the spoken or written word of their deepest and most secret desires.

Nighttime dreams and daydreams together contain full and complete expressions of the special tensions inherent in the life of the unconscious. All that has to be done to understand them is to work harder at the task of expressing them. Normally this task stops when the dreamer considers his internal dreams to be refined enough for external expression, and so to be the source of action. At that stage it is safe to act without the risk of unexpected explosions from hidden perverse tendencies. Now is the time when individuals are ready to make contact with members of the opposite sex and to express their feelings freely. As these feelings are no longer dangerous, the time is ripe for approaching the man or woman who seems most likely to make an ideal partner.

In the next few chapters we shall see that even when effective contact has been made, sex life is not entirely free from aggressive tendencies, and in both partners some hostility is still mingled with tenderness. However, in most cases the actual amount of hostility is so small as to be harmless. If this is not so, and the two partners have not succeeded in dissolving most of their internal aggressions, the couple is likely to have a hard time at the beginning of their life together. Most societies have been wise in advising young people not to rush into either formal or informal unions, suggesting fairly long engagements in preparation for permanent union, and even advising a period of abstinence from sexual relations. Age-long experience has shown that if the latent aggression is not dissolved in advance, sex relations will turn sour and leave nothing but the bitterness which accompanies any act, but especially the sex act, when there is hostility or fear. Initiation rites, which are well known to be universal (far from being an exception, the Western world spreads them over a number of years in schools and churches), are usually very cruel and provide a harsh test for the boys or girls compelled to undergo them. But it may be asked whether they are not really magical devices for dissolving latent aggression, or dramatic games providing situations in line with the desires and fears of the unconscious in the most striking possible way. Their twofold purpose would be to prevent such eruptions in the future and to purge the persons concerned of the most aggressive aspects of their sexuality. Obviously the initiate must prove that he possesses qualities that will be useful in adult life, or that he will be able to protect his group or his family (wife and children) from outside dangers and supply them with food. But this obvious meaning of the initiation rites does not seem to be the only one, and it does not take into account certain symbolic mutilation or castration ceremonies. I believe that the real explanation is that these rites are intended to separate aggression from sexuality, so that an individual entering the adult world may use the former for defending his wife, his future children and his group, and the latter entirely for procreation and enjoyment. In other words, the purpose of the rites is to purify the content of the unconscious, not by elimination, but by analysis, sorting out the aggressive elements from the sexual ones.

In any event, it seems to me that the daily and nightly dreams of human beings fulfill this analytical role. By holding the unconscious and the preconscious responsible for the development of all kinds of psychic paralyses, psychoanalysts have unwittingly helped to spread the erroneous belief that they are evil and should be avoided like the plague. The error has arisen from a confusion between the content of the unconscious, which is assuredly demoniacal, and its function, which is just as assuredly constructive.

I should like at this point to see how far we have gone. We started with a perverse sexual impulse, triggered by individuals who stimulated the beholder but refused to satisfy him. First improvement: the urges are directed toward an internal object and become latent, thus sparing the person concerned and others the dangers of real action. Second improvement: to prevent the perverse impulses from turning into a more powerful and dangerous force than a mere organic reaction, a prohibitory and legislative Superego develops to hold down these impulses and compel them to conform to rules and accept compromises. Third improvement: as it is likely to upset the individual's equilibrium, the tension between tendencies and prohibitions has to be resolved. It cannot be resolved in action, since all attempts at action are forbidden. Faced with the unendurable struggle between "yes" and "no," all that can be done is to project the tension onto an internal screen, called the imagination, where the latent conflicts can be expressed and analyzed and the personality prepared to meet reality.

At the point we have reached, individuals, both male and female, have their own conscious dreams; these are the product of a long distillation of the crude data furnished by the unconscious and are a precious substance that gives its own flavor to budding sentimental relationships. The benefit of all the work achieved is clear: aggressive acts have been restrained; perverse tendencies have not led to any disastrous action; internal tension has been relieved; and, above all, the sex drives have begun to lose their corrosive elements. Approaches to a mate can safely be undertaken. People no longer feel themselves to be dangerous, and so they do not feel so threatened by their peers.

IV

THE EXPRESSION OF
UNCONSCIOUS SEXUALITY:
NARCISSISM

To capture the attention of the female, the peacock spreads its fan and unfolds its plumage as wide as it will go, thus becoming more visible and increasing its chances of causing erotic stimulation. What can human beings do? To start with, they have the same means at their disposal as other animals: blood pressure, muscular tension, body poise, tone of voice, even the smell of sweat. But there are also others that they have invented: perfumes enhance their natural odor; they improve their voices through singing and their body poise by dancing; they use cosmetics to set off the natural colors of the skin. This systematic heightening of the natural stimulants, in which humans display great ingenuity, enables them to go further than any other members of the animal world. Looked at in this way the only difference between humans and animals seems to be one of variety. The means of attracting the opposite sex open to most animal species are transmitted from one generation to the next without any great change, while humans vary and adjust their methods in almost infinite profusion, from one period, place and age to another. There is no end to the quirks of human fashion.

But the difference between humans and animals is not merely one of degree; there is also a qualitative element. For, paradoxically, while the range of devices available is virtually unlimited, it is rare for men and women to use them to the full immediately on experiencing erotic stimulation. In adolescence and even later, they are shy, unnatural in their attitude and voice, unable to act or express themselves freely. Of course there are exceptions, but even the most self-confident men and women require some practice, even if only a little. What I wrote earlier about inhibitions and the internalization of impulses explains why, and I shall not make the point again. But it will be interesting to examine the ways human beings handle their perverse tendencies, inhibitions and dreams.

By a twist which shows how remarkable nature is, something that was originally a disadvantage is gradually turned into an asset. The same perverse sexuality, whose effects on the hidden psyche we have already discussed, and which should by all accounts be repulsive to any potential mate, in fact takes on forms which act as erotic stimuli, so that resistance melts away and gives place to invitation.

This brings me to the most important qualitative difference between animals and human beings: *human beings possess means of expression.* When a peacock spreads its fan it is not expressing anything. Even anthropomorphically speaking, it would be wrong to say that it is expressing desire. The organic tension that leads to the magnificent display of plumage is merely reaction: it is in no way expression. It is only a phase in the chain of actions and reactions that will bring a male together with a female in heat, and it lasts only a moment. All that it hides is a series of physiological transformations related to the state of the metabolism, the temperature and the light at the particular moment. There is no previous desire underlying it. Only human beings are capable of expressive actions, that is to say, acts and words revealing the hidden pressure of the dreams and fears of the unconscious.

1

Here are three examples to show the difference between actions that provide direct stimulation and those that are expressive. The first example is very ordinary and taken from daily life. Any man with a little taste makes a clear distinction between women who are merely pretty or elegant and women whose beauty or elegance lies in their mode of expression. On the one hand, the merely pretty woman is perhaps no more than a splendid female with naturally attractive features "improved" by human artifice. Having no complexes or any inner life, she is really like the peacock I described above. Most men will say that she is superficial or shallow. It is not that she is unattractive to them; indeed, she is likely to have the greatest success with the most complicated and tortured souls among them, simply because she offers simplicity and the promise of relaxation without complications. She herself is quite unable to understand any of their difficulties, since she has only just enough intelligence to exploit her own charms. On the other hand, the expressive woman, who has perhaps fewer physical charms than the other, has eyes sparkling with life; even her hands evoke fear or hope; her lips frame words that add to her mystery. Her whole body is a medium of expression, but her beauty will not be fully revealed at first, or even second, glance. Only close attention will lead to the discovery that she is the embodiment of an unconscious destiny. She is like André Breton's Nadja: "We sat down on the terrace of a café near the Gare du Nord. I looked at her more closely. What was so special about her eyes? What combination of obscure distress and luminous pride was mirrored there?"[1] She is like John Cowper Powys' Perdita Wane: "Perdita was neither a plain girl, nor a pretty girl. . . . The corners of her mouth, one of those mouths that find it so difficult to remain patiently closed, but must always be expressing some sort of intense feeling by their tremblings, were now drawn down in a woe-begone droop. Her chin was undoubtedly the weakest feature in her face; and in the light of that ship's lantern she allowed it to assume a helplessness and a hopelessness that would have disappeared in a moment had anyone addressed her. Then would have become more emphatic, as she raised her head, a certain proud curve in her nose, not to speak of a thoughtful dignity in her clear-cut brow, above which, beneath the rim of her hat, her brown waves. . . ."[2] To take a male example, there is the chief character of the same novel, Skald, nicknamed the Jobber because his job was to carry all sorts of goods around the country in his motorboat, "Cormorant," and his truck, the "Snail." He was about thirty-five years old, physically very strong, but eccentric and secretive, living very much by himself and possessed of a personal magnetism that made him the best-known man on the coast.

These characters from literature bring me to my second example, which is pathological rather than psychological. This is the extraordinary attraction that criminals, per-

[1] André Breton, *Nadja,* Paris, Gallimard, 19e ed., pp. 79–80.
[2] John Cowper Powys, *Weymouth Sands,* New York, Simon and Schuster, 1934, p. 29.

verts or madmen have for some women. As can be seen from the diaries of criminals who have set down their impressions of prison life, it is quite common for men whose crimes have made them notorious to receive proposals from women who wish to live with them when they come out of prison. Nor is it rare for sufferers from schizophrenia, who are often brilliant talkers, to arouse fierce passions in women. It will be said no doubt that it is the maternal instinct that makes women want to come to the rescue of these tragic beings officially rejected by society. While this may be partly true, it is not the whole explanation. Can the women really have so little perception that they are not aware of the dangers they run, and so persist in the mistaken belief that these poor souls can be saved? The humanitarian and maternal motives are surely *post-hoc* inventions, indicating an attraction for which the real reasons are to be sought in the unconscious and the laws of erotic seduction. If women lose their sense of reality to such a degree, they must be under some kind of spell. The explanation does in fact seem to be that pathological or criminal careers are such accurate reflections of the unconscious dramas of the human soul that they become sexually stimulating. Both crime and madness, raw products of psychic tension, may take on erotic qualities. If they have a certain amount of flair and a gift for the spectacular, criminals and madmen become attractive instead of repulsive. When they discover men whose careers are so much in keeping with the dictates of their own unconscious, some women cannot rest until they have made contact with them. We need not go so far as to look for our examples in extremes and exceptions: the sensational, the melodramatic, the sordid—all can achieve as much success as honest and principled work, as long as they have "style." All this goes to prove that however monstrous or misshapen they may be, the unconscious can indeed manifest itself in exciting effects quite different in quality from those produced by simple biological stimuli, and that we would do well not to ignore them.

My last example is more technical, and it should be of particular interest to psychoanalysts and others who read the literature. These people know not only that the patient undergoing psychoanalytical treatment soon reaches the position where he has to stave off alarming feelings about his analyst, but that the same is true in reverse of the analyst. Unless he is made of steel, he soon develops powerful feelings about the patient, whom he has pressed to speak as openly as possible. This is the phenomenon of countertransference, the exact counterpart of the transference experienced by the patient. Is the explanation to be found entirely in the psychoanalyst's unconscious? Not necessarily, if we are prepared to admit that the verbal description of the patient's intimate conflicts is itself both expressive and erotic. Especially when the patient, who may well be rather hysterical, pumps out his red-hot confidences, he acquires a sort of fascination which the psychoanalyst would be quite wrong to ignore. It is of course true that the fascination is to some extent explained by the fact that the analyst's unconscious is like the patient's. But it has also to be accepted that the patient's expression of the contents of his unconscious—conflicts between sexuality and aggression, pleasure and prohibition—can themselves become stimuli and reinforce the simpler stimuli of form, color and odor.

We have already seen that most criminals, perverts and neurotics are unable to express themselves. Their tragedy is that they are forced to have recourse to real acts in order to exorcise their demons. At least, this is one side of the explanation of their behavior; the other is connected with the disproportionate amount of hostility in the sexuality-aggressiveness mix. Normally, when the conflicts are not too acute and the individual is accustomed to substituting symbolic acts for real ones, images for things and words for deeds, aggression can be dispersed spontaneously and harmlessly in expression. There are two advantages in this: not only does expressing himself relieve the sufferer, it also adds to his sexual attractiveness. Those who are still unconvinced should consider the successes in love of people whose job it is to produce pleasure by one or another form of expression—poets, musicians, acrobats, dancers and the like.

2

Dark and secret ideas may be expressed by any of the means of which the body is capable: sounds, movements, colors or words. But regardless of the form of expression, the basic requirements for conveying these ideas are the same. First, the manifestations of the unconscious are erotic and stimulating only if they are something more than a mere reflection of reality. A straightforward scientific statement is not at all exciting, while the scientist's life story may be tense and exciting enough in itself to create emotion. An objective description in the neutral terms used by a physiologist or psychologist can excite only a maniac, for whom even the most abstract symbols or numerals may be a source of "ideas." Generally speaking, we may say that any strictly "factual" statement, that is to say, one whose sole purpose is to provide information, is unlikely to retain much of the erotic content characteristic of any expression that has just emerged from the unconscious. Even the most realistic literature is in some way different from a scientific treatise. The earliest manifestations of the unconscious are not straightforward, cold or brutal statements about sex. And a work of art ceases to fascinate if the only thing it expresses is a desire for sexual relations. In art, everything is symbolic, as indeed it should be, and we should not forget that human beings live by symbols before they enter the real world.

In our dreams, that is to say, at the preconscious level, the conflicts between sexuality and aggression, perverse pleasure and prohibition are not expressed in objective images but in a form that may be called caricature. Up to the point we have now reached, sex life has been so mixed with aggression and internal opposition that the mind has been unable to form any objective idea of it. When suffering adolescents or schizophrenic adults picture to themselves the struggle between the forces of love and hate in the world, or between the strict rule of law and the appeals of desire, they are still a long way from thinking of sex acts as such. The sex instinct is still too bound up with painful components for pleasure to be reconcilable with the social order or for it to be imagined in its most specific form.

In every field of activity, but particularly in those related to the senses, objectivity—meaning a respectful attention to reality—comes not at the beginning but at the end of the developmental process. The beginning of sex life is marked not by objectivity but by erotic excitement. It is only much later that, if all goes well, we find two people whose intense interest in each other is expressed by complete abandonment of self. Between these two extremes—one hardly perceptible and buried in the bowels of physiology, the other a supreme human ideal—people undergo all sorts of internal changes and work through a long process of trial and error. Their sex life is disordered and uneven; it is never openly referred to, and shows itself only in symbolic forms representing an unconscious past and confused promises of a better world beyond the reach of art or words.

Why is it that so many books on love and conjugal happiness are so boring and leave the reader with such a feeling of emptiness? Perhaps because of the authors' tactical error in believing they can induce people to progress by showing them an ideal goal. Worse still, they seem to need these idyllic descriptions to maintain their own and other peoples' illusions about themselves, as if mankind could achieve love by wanting it and talking about it enough. The great artists who never talk about perfect love (how dull they would be if they did!), but who describe the internal struggle between tenderness and brutality in symbolic terms, are doing mankind a greater service.

Freud has explained that the purpose of psychoanalysis is to make conscious that which was originally unconscious. This process need not be undertaken only as a form of treatment. Indeed, it goes on all the time, in all of us. Only in those cases where the strength of deep-seated pressures makes it painful or difficult is recourse to a healer necessary. It is made easier by all those people who have set themselves the task of describing some part of the pain of human desires. Their help is particularly valuable when they do not so much give warnings about actual behavior as concentrate on expressing the forms and drives of the unconscious.

I said earlier that to be erotic, works of expression must be less a description of objective reality than of subjective reality and of the way—dramatic, comic or lyric—in which a human being feels and lives through his internal conflicts. We now have to answer the question, How does this expression actually take place?

I shall try to explain by an analogy with the phenomenon of lightning. For the real question to be answered is, What can produce these wonderful sudden flashes that light up the darkness of the unconscious? The unconscious may be compared to a high-tension area with positive and negative poles, the nuclei described in the previous chapter. These poles give off sudden flashes whenever objects that are good conductors come between them. The resulting discharges both light up the poles, or nuclei, which emit them and help to reduce the original charges.

There is no lack of good conductors either in nature or in history. A vast army caught on the ice, a crevasse opening onto an enchanted cave, a public figure slipping on a banana skin, a house painter who becomes one of the most powerful dictators in history, Cleopatra's nose, a girl's breasts or a forbidden fruit—any of these may cause a discharge between the poles of the unconscious mind.

André Breton's surrealist theories are important for having at least shown that there was no need to invent good conductors of mental energy in the form of reasonably acceptable ready-made metaphors concocted by poets: one need only look around in one's room or in the street to find plenty of useful ones in the guise of striking coincidences or chance happenings. The surrealist movement will fade out like any other vogue, but it will leave behind a better understanding of art as an expression of the forces in the unconscious. Indeed, we already have a better understanding of the artist's role. In whatever field he works, he seeks out the best conductors of mental energy, and polishes them and turns them into instruments devoted henceforth entirely to the service of the emotions.

3

After this digression on the nature of the means of expression available to human beings, I should like to return to the development of sexuality, and see the uses to which these means are put. This way of wording the problem is not really satisfactory, as it would seem to assume a two-sided phenomenon, with a well-established inner sex life and an outer part which is a sort of wardrobe containing a number of costumes for external show. But I shall let the metaphor stand, crude though it is, as it does serve to spotlight the error I wish to expose: that human sexuality with its desires, its tendencies and its fears exists from the beginning as a fully formed part of the psyche. I cannot emphasize often enough that sexuality is built up gradually, even imperceptibly, first by internal development of the instinctive reactions and later (and this is the point at which we have now arrived) by external expression of the products of this internal development. A person's sex life will be worthy of him as a human being only if the initial erotic stimulation has undergone this dual process of internalization and external expression. I have already dealt with internalization, and will now discuss external expression.

It is here that I want to introduce the concept of the "good conductor"—an object, event, or person whose characteristics are such as to permit the unconscious to discharge its tensions. The unconscious finds many such conductors in the real world; and by investing their ambiguous character with emotional significance, uses them to set off a flash between the internal poles. And here we come to one of the fundamental concepts of psychoanalysis, known as cathexis *(Besetzung)*. The image covered by this concept was so obvious to the early psychoanalysts that they saw no reason to justify it. They were so preoccupied with watching the development of the cathexis of libidinal energy in a person of the same sex, in one of the opposite sex, or in the individual himself that they would have thought it a waste of time to stop and think about the image itself. Personally, I have no hesitation in spending some time on this point, as I hope in so doing to avoid the misunderstandings that so frequently arise between psychoanalysts and other knowledgeable people, and to give a better description of the individual's progress toward a fully flowering sexual life.

The concept of cathexis has no meaning except in relation to the psyche, where there is a tension between opposites and a need for objects to release that tension. It has no meaning at the very simple level of the instincts, which can be understood simply on the basis of the laws of excitement and response, action and reaction, or the trigger mechanisms. When psychoanalysts talk of cathexis in connection with sexual or aggressive instincts they would seem to be using the term carelessly. Cathexis is always related to the unconscious or the preconscious. It does occur, though very feebly, and even furtively, in the production of dreams, since they contain the images, memories and perceptions which seem to be attracted and organized by the tension of the unconscious. The cathexis becomes clear and intense when the hidden psychic tension moves from simply attracting bits and pieces of perception and memory to selecting from among real things. At this point a human being becomes something like a walking high-tension transformer which moves about seeking good conductors, and releasing discharges through the most malleable and compatible components of reality, thus giving them a luster that they do not possess in themselves.

The objects of such investment by the unconscious (considered as tension between aggressiveness and sexuality, pleasure and prohibition) are neither people who are without pasts nor stable, wise and happy people, but those who are ambiguous. At the risk of boring my readers, let me offer some obvious examples, such as the attraction for simple souls—and some part of us always remains simple— of kings and princes, queens and film stars, all of whom bear the most obvious signs of contradiction. They call up ideas of intense pleasure, luxury and self-indulgence, but these pleasures are not for ordinary mortals, and are therefore prohibited. Consider, too, the fascination that most adolescents find both in public figures who preach, whether sincerely or not, an ideal of justice and love, and those who seem to be incarnations of tyranny. Finally, consider the popularity of those spectator sports in which life and death are separated only by a hair's breadth; they are particularly exciting because they are the finest examples of the tension between the desire for success and the fear of failure, between the ultimate in human effort and the immediacy of death.

My readers may be irritated at finding here only contrasts in black and white, rather dull opposing pairs apparently derived from the so-called dualist system of thought. But the blame should be placed on the nature of the unconscious and the preconscious. Private dreams, popular legends and age-old myths testify to the dualistic nature of the products of the human imagination. Among these contrasting pairs, in the realm of sex, there is one well known to all adolescents and some adults: on the one hand the loose woman leading a promiscuous life or even a harlot's existence, confessing no faith and obedient to no law; on the other, the noble wife and mother, the guardian of both faith and law. And these two contrasting types of women themselves contain further contradictions: prostitutes may offer pleasure, but deprive their clients of honor; wives may provide a home and status, but deprive their spouse of sexual satisfaction. It is genuinely difficult for many people to believe that a prostitute can have a soul or a wife-mother can have desires. And yet the truth is generally not black and white, but gray. It is the unconscious which accentuates the difference and turns a quantitative difference into a qualitative one. The prostitute and the wife-mother are sisters, similar in many ways. The only difference is in the quantity in which their qualities exist. But the unconscious will not have anything to do with these nice distinctions. It sees only the surface, and when it finds sharp contrasts it uses them for expression and for discharging tensions.

That is why unconscious sexuality begins by attaching itself to distant, inaccessible beings who are known only by their pictures, like heroes and film stars. It takes plenty of courage to go up to someone directly and ask him or her to be an object of cathexis or investment, and thus become involved in the hero-worshiper's private life. It is only prudent to start with unreal people—characters from literature, the cinema or history—or impersonal symbols of virility or femininity. This is the whole meaning of sexual daydreams. For in them there are bits of reality—breasts, hair or legs which belong to no one in particular, declarations that reach the ear of no living man or woman, lascivious events that take place in vague, nonexistent places—a mixture of pleasure and torment that has no counterpart in real life. In this changing, strictly interior, though conscious, world we shall find the chief internal objects of the unconscious life masquerading as real things. It is an imaginary world that forms the link between the unconscious and reality, and represents a crystallization of fragmented objects around the fear- and desire-laden elements of the unconscious.

A remarkable thing—and I doubt whether psychologists have paid enough attention to it—is that a love affair generally begins as the result of some exciting group activity. Erotic feelings can develop at any time—in the street, in the office, in class—anywhere where the two sexes are together. But for two people to declare their feelings to each other, special conditions are needed, and these are not merely a social but a psychological necessity. There is resistance to be overcome, and this is achieved more naturally and easily coming out of the theater or at the end of a dance or party than at other times. When the whole population of Melanesian villages is dancing to the music of drums at nightfall, couples steal away into the bush to consummate the emotions stirred up by the festivities. And every human celebration that is at all dramatic or marks an unusual event also reflects the inner tension of the participants. Communal events give them both the right and the opportunity to express themselves, and this always involves a release of the sexual instinct. Even the most ordinary evening entertainments, with dancing, coarse or subtle double-talk, a warm atmosphere and the flow of alcohol, lead to a rise in the emotional level and hence represent a partial projection of the unconscious of everyone present. And so we should not be surprised if they lead to declarations, either on the spot or later, that would be out of the question in ordinary circumstances.

Naturally, I would never claim that all human celebrations are merely erotic. They also contain sacred and dramatic elements. Village wakes are always connected with the main feasts in the church calendar. When they celebrate important historical dates (avoidance of a plague, the end of a war, performance of a miracle), they represent and symbolize the human drama, the struggle of good and evil, of life and death. But as they are in a sense theatrical games, they cannot help being involved with pleasure and hence with erotic desire. And this is why couples prolong the effect of the release of their emotions and so spontaneously speak the words and perform the acts of physical love, either during or after the festivities themselves. This is perhaps the best illustration of the erotic nature of expressions of the unconscious.

That people require special circumstances reflecting the lightning flashes of the unconscious before they can engage in emotional and sexual relationships proves three things: first, that they have to purge themselves of all the complex reactions arising from the crude erotic stimulus; second, that the expression of these reactions, which are a combination of desire and fear (like the forward and backward movements of dance steps), itself becomes a sexual stimulant; and third, that it is not so easy as it might seem for a human being to make serious advances to a desirable partner. There are, of course, great differences between individuals—between the unthinking playboy who smashes through any obstacles and the blushing youth wondering how he will explain to his beloved a quarter of what he feels. But in any event, at least a minimum of internal development and symbolic expression is required. It is only after a lapse of time that varies with age, temperament and the intensity of the inner drives that individuals shed their symbols and direct their emotions toward a *flesh-and-blood* being. And even then, they will not at first direct this emotional energy toward a stranger or someone outside themselves; they will use a being intimately connected with themselves, in other words, their own person. This is the phenomenon known as narcissism.

4

Until now, we have been speaking of those aspects of the external world through which human beings can express their sexuality. But in a sense, this expression is passive: all that the individual does is to direct his interest, which wells up from the depths of the unconscious, toward any object, event or person that appears dramatic and in tune with his own inner conflict. Sooner or later, depending on his character and experience, he will cease to be merely passive and will give erotic value to two things that are most clearly his, that is, his body and his soul. Narcissism is nothing else but this.

We have here a new and important stage in the development of sexual relations; but while it is a positive advance in relation to earlier stages (withdrawal, perverse auto-eroticism), we are still far from the establishment of any final sexual link.

Superficially speaking, narcissism consists of sexual love directed to the lover himself or herself. If we delve more deeply, however, we shall see that it is a form of real behavior enabling people to examine and organize their egos, that is to say, all their physical and mental characteristics taken together, in order to make themselves agreeable and seductive. Narcissism is a form of behavior rather than a form of love. It is a way of composing an image of oneself. People organize themselves in a certain way, then stand back to see what effect they produce on themselves, hoping that the effect on others will be the same. It is as if they were going through a solitary rehearsal of a seduction scene. The whole purpose is to make the body and the whole personality an instrument of self-expression, and hence an object for investment by the psychic forces of potential mates.

Freud was well aware that narcissism always contains some intention of creating sympathetic magic.[3] Its aim is to create an effect and achieve an indirect influence over others. Looked at in this way, narcissistic behavior represents a real advance on unconscious and preconscious auto-eroticism, and even on the passive behavior which consists of merely accepting the liberating effect of expressive objects chosen from nature or history. It is a step toward reality. While people at this stage do not actually appear on the stage of social life, they are at least preparing for it, like actors rehearsing their lines in front of a mirror or in

[3] Sigmund Freud, *Zur Einführung des Narzissmus*, G.W., vol. x, p. 140.

the wings. Of course, this sort of preparation for seduction may last for months or years if people are too timid to go on stage or undertake a real relationship. This is the moment to recall the general law of human development, which is that however great an advance a new phase may be in relation to inner development, it will become pathological if it lasts too long or if it prevents further development.

We must now try to see what progress is achieved in moving from the mere passivity of spontaneous emotional investment to narcissism. We have seen that, virtually without any assistance from the person concerned, psychic tensions discharge on the most expressive people and things within the field of perception. Before any action is undertaken to make a real approach to an attractive mate, an intermediate step—narcissism—is needed to enable the active party to make himself or herself as expressive and hence as erotic as possible. People in this stage are no longer satisfied with watching their unconscious fight out its conflicts in front of their eyes. They will try to express in their own person the latent struggle between sexuality and aggressiveness, between desire and prohibition. By thus allowing the main latent psychic tensions to show through their now expressive Ego, they give it a glow like that of a work of art or a symbolic figure.

In this connection it is worth considering the one-person dances of primitive peoples. In African bars, individuals dancing by and for themselves are a common sight. A mirror reflects their movements, which express violence and abandonment, desire and refusal in a sort of wordless play. The dancers are in fact busy organizing and improving the expressive elements of their bodies. It is as if they were carried away by their unconscious, which is trying to assume physical form through the muscles of the face, limbs and body. What becomes gradually visible is an intense sexuality together with all its accompanying manifestations of fear, anxiety and victorious joy. All the unconscious forms of sexuality come to the surface and are exposed in the dance rhythms, both fast and slow. Individuals thus work out under their own critical gaze the pattern of sexual signals intended to cast a spell on anyone seeking expressive objects, or, as I have called them above, good conductors of inner psychic tension, in the outside world.

In the tribes I have visited, these narcissistic, magical dances are performed by men and women, by young and old alike. Even when couples danced together, I had the impression that this was only an imitation of the white Western world, and that, psychologically speaking, the partners were not a couple; each individual was concerned mainly with himself and his own gyrations. And this has led me to wonder whether our modern dances, with one man embracing one woman, are not late products of civilization made possible by the intensive flowering of subjectivity and intersubjectivity. In most human societies, dancing is performed either by individuals or by groups and the main aim is always to make as much magic as possible and to render the body as sensitive as it can be to the rhythms of the unconscious psychic tension.

In our society, magical narcissistic dances survive only as choreography, but mirrors are still used for dressing and makeup. Girls spend plenty of time in front of the mirror, especially when preparing for dates. This, too, is narcissism, a tryout of the effect of the body. But in addition to these elementary expressions, narcissistic love takes more subtle and sophisticated forms. In his difficult but rewarding work on narcissism, Freud grouped them together under an activity he called *Idealbildung:* the creation of an Ego ideal. Under the influence of social pressure, individuals make up interesting personalities for themselves and continually measure their actions and desires against an ideal that grows up almost unnoticed within them. The praiseworthy practice of self-criticism may be one way of at least partially filling this need for narcissistic observation and of satisfying the desire to create the image of the Ego most admired by the group in which one lives.

It is worth analyzing the symbolic content of the personality narcissists seek to find in their mental or physical mirrors. Most of the features of this ideal stem naturally from the value judgments of the environment. They reflect the behavior and qualities current in a society at any given moment. But whatever the source of these features, we must try to understand their secret symbolism.

In the example I mentioned above, the African dancing alone in front of a mirror in a bar, the symbolism is obvious: stylized gestures representing violence and aggressiveness are followed by gestures just as stylized representing gentleness, abandonment and union. Leaving aside the infinitely variable details and shades of meaning, we shall always find in addition to allusions to sexual relations in the ordinary sense, an affirmation of the triumph of love over hate, of confidence over fear, of love's embrace over sadistic destruction. The personality put together by girls sitting at their mirrors is often provocative, for the most erotic elements of the body are both emphasized and hidden. This is a stylized science, so subtle as to be hardly noticeable, by which the body is concealed just enough to exacerbate desire. It is a cruel game of hide and seek, which will not last forever, it is well understood, but is a preliminary to self-abandonment. It is in the idea of provocation that we find one of the clearest meanings of narcissism.

People invent personalities for themselves, thus projecting into the real world sexual desire and refusal, impulses and the repression of impulses, perversion (aggressive sexuality) and love (satisfying sexuality). By making one's body and Ego a channel for the expression of inner struggles, one gives them an added touch of sexual attractiveness, adding a new bloom, plucked from the depths of the unconscious, to the features that make one naturally seductive.

Will this analysis stand up when applied to the Ego ideal of Freudian theory? At first sight it would seem not. This Ego ideal is described by Freud as the most powerful force that keeps sexual tendencies repressed. For him it is like a condensation of all the cultural and moral norms passed on by adults, of whom parents are the most important. Or, it is like an incarnation of all the perfectionist desires haunting parents and society (including teachers, educators and public opinion alike). In short, instead of being a more subtle way of making the Ego erotic, or a first step toward escaping from unconscious perverse auto-eroticism, is it just the opposite, that is, the main factor in repressing those desires that may not decently reach the light of day?

Freud clearly understood that this analysis, which dates back to 1914, was inadequate, since in 1923 he found it necessary to supersede or complement the concept of the Ego ideal by that of the Superego as the psychic source of repression. As we have seen, this repression starts from an identification of the unconscious with the prohibitory forces of society. In these circumstances is the concept of the Ego ideal of no significance? Not at all. Once we stop attributing to it a defensive and repressive function, we can obtain a clearer idea of its positive role.

Freud's analysis has shown us the way. The purpose of this ideal, he says, is to meet the demands of primary narcissism, through which children wish to be loved unreservedly by their parents, and more especially by their mother. Let us look more closely at this desire to be approved and loved by someone just as we were by our father or mother in the first years of our life. We see quite clearly from this that narcissistic behavior is part of the process of increasing erotic attractiveness.

It is a common mistake to take too abstract a view of the Ego ideal, or to consider it as a static object unrelated to movements in the psyche, and to believe that it contains only desires for perfection, generosity and self-denial. In actual fact, narcissistic behavior is much more complex than this. Let us go back to the example of self-criticism, which inevitably involves a confrontation between the honest and the dishonest, the perverse and the good, egoism and generosity. What is important is not primarily or exclusively the ways in which such a self-examination is resolved, but the picture we paint for ourselves of our mind and its tensions, so that we can deliberately perform some magical action on a force we consider transcendental, e.g., God for the believer, public opinion or something similar for the nonbeliever. It is often said that this introspective review of the self is in fact an act of awareness: a crystallization, in the form of stereotyped images and well-defined concepts, of internal reactions which had hitherto been experienced only rather vaguely, in a sort of marginal awareness. And is this crystallization not very similar to the stylization of features and gestures sought after by the dancers I mentioned earlier? Anyone who undertakes self-examination is undertaking genuine inner development. He borrows various gestures from his early life, turns them into stylized gestures of hate and love and so creates an image of himself whose primary purpose is to make himself agreeable to other humans or to God. Any thought of improving his behavior in the real world is only secondary, as can be proved by the frequent inefficacy in this respect of many hours of introspection.

Freud has defined narcissism as a libidinal investment

of the Ego, *eine Libidobesetzung des Ichs*.[4] How is this unusual definition to be understood? The Ego, as we agreed at the beginning of this book, is the organization of our mental and bodily functions. Now, this organization can become an object of attachment, i.e., a good conductor of deep-seated psychic tensions. Since in this way it becomes a means of expression for the unconscious, it also takes on magical and erotic significance. We can therefore consider the Ego ideal as the real Ego exploited for libidinal purposes. The bodily and mental functions are used for magical and expressive ends. This does not mean that the Ego is invested by pure sexual energy, but rather that it attracts to itself the varied and contradictory contents of the unconscious for erotic purposes in general. The term *libido* refers not so much to the energy flowing into a personality as to the purpose of this operation, which is to pour into the personality the contents of the unconscious in all their force and richness. It would be taking too narrow a view to speak only of an occupation of the Ego by libidinal or sexual energy. For it is not merely the sex instinct, taken in the narrow sense, that an individual draws into himself; it is all the unconscious and the preconscious, containing both sexual desires and aggression, both tendencies to pleasure and fear of prohibition, that use the personality, the real Ego as a means of self-expression and stylization, thus acquiring greater erotic force. In narcissism, all the drives of the unconscious try to obtain possession of every one of the Ego's characteristics, or looked at the other way around, the person concerned relaxes the traits of his physical and mental being to allow the tension of his deepest, innermost organisms to show through. In short, he increases the psychic attractiveness of both his body and his Ego.

[4] *Ibid.*, p. 141.

Narcissus admiring his reflection in the lake is not satisfied with just looking at himself. He is trying to improve on the features of his face and body. And this he is unable to do merely by smiling or adopting alluring postures. This would merely be stupid. What he actually does is to run through the whole gamut of attitudes and postures expressing rebellion, discontent, hope and joy one after the other. The game he is playing in the waters of the lake is by no means dull or repetitive, as it covers every possible emotion and feeling. Narcissus is in fact charging his body with emotional energy, and making it sufficiently pliable to react to the slightest sign—from the unconscious. The Freudian theory of narcissism has been understood too narrowly, as if Narcissus were merely in love with his own body. Taken in this way the theory leaves out of account all those actions by which Narcissus could hope to express emotions other than love, such as rage, despair and suffering. For the narcissist is trying to bring all the events of his inner life to the surface of his own body, in order to make it as erotically attractive as possible.

5

The phrase "his own body," used to describe the primary area for the manifestation of tensions by the unconscious, should not be taken too narrowly. For it does not refer merely to the anatomical structure, it covers the whole personality—external appearance, qualities of voice and vision, language and ideas. It is the whole Ego, with all its facilities for adapting itself to circumstance, that is the vehicle for expression. Nevertheless, it is still true that the body plays a predominant role because it is both solid and enduring. This is perhaps an illustration of the Latin tag *verba volant, corpus manet,* meaning words are lost on the

wind but the body remains. Words are continually changing into ideas, and ideas into words, and there is no way of
holding onto them, while the body in the narrow sense is
always there with all its qualities and defects, with its own
individual shape and organs. And this is no doubt why as
sexuality develops, people's interests tend to shift from
the things of the mind to the things of the body. Very early
on, certain parts of the body—mouth and lips, breasts,
thighs and buttocks—begin to receive special attention.

The attention devoted to the most obvious or suggestive
parts of the body in the narcissistic phase is not merely due
to the desire to enhance the attractiveness of the organs
that provide biological stimuli. The situation is more complicated than this. A peacock opening its fan devotes its
whole attention to the peahen and none to its own body;
but a human being also thinks of himself and his body. He
may be completely absorbed in it, as in the legend of Narcissus, and as in the case of those sexually obsessed people
whose masturbations are accompanied by intense visions
of their body or some part of it. Not only does every suggestive detail of the anatomy become a hook on which to
hang a projection of the unconscious, but often, at least
in extreme narcissism, every phase of heterosexual love
play is played out on a person's own body, one part acting
as a male organ, another as a female organ, without his being aware of it. Even if there is no perverse action, a given
part of the body may have special virtues in its owner's eyes
because it provides a particularly easy channel for expression by the unconscious and the imagination. For example,
a young woman attached excessive importance to her hairstyle. She had long and not unattractive hair which she
wore not loose but rolled up in a bun, which made her
look rather fierce. She very much wanted to have it cut, but
was afraid that if she did so, she would lose her father's
admiration. It is no exaggeration to say that the battle of

the hair reflected this young lady's basic conflict: First, she wanted to be a man, her hair being a substitute for the male organ and a symbol of strength, as in the story of Samson and Delilah. But then she also wanted to be a woman, although this desire was accompanied by fear that to be a woman meant being diminished and mutilated. Finally, she suffered from a mixture of desire and fear in connection with her father's love, for he might well have found the replacement of the bun by a more feminine hairstyle upsetting for his own equilibrium.

Nothing is more extraordinary than the way in which any striking feature of the human body can be laden with psychological significance reflecting the workings of the unconscious. I would even go so far as to say that a feature never has a merely operative function; it also has a symbolic role that becomes more or less definite, depending on the intensity of the conflicts taking place in the person at the time. Even the hairs in a man's beard—and what can be more ordinary than that!—can become a sign of virility, or even virility itself, to the extent that some impotent depressives find shaving the beard an erotic act leading to erection and ejaculation. This example is of course pathological, but it does clearly illustrate two points: First, the physical representation of the idea that sexuality is a threat to physical integrity can itself exert a powerful erotic effect. Second, this idea may attach itself in the most unexpected manner to any parts of the body, even nonsexual ones, if they express some conflict in the unconscious. To go back to the analogy I used earlier, at the end of the narcissistic phase of development, of all the objects to be found in nature, a person's own body becomes the best conductor of inner psychic tensions.

The benefits of this erotization of the body or somatization of perverse sexuality are very great. The original inhibitions that were the starting point for the process of internalization and the development of the psychic side of sexuality succeeded only in desexualizing the body. The narcissistic representation of inner conflicts has the opposite effect: for the body, profiting from all the changes that take place during narcissistic development, receives so much attention that the most sensitive parts also become the most expressive and the most laden with symbolism.

Narcissists become interested in the sex organs only after a considerable lapse of time, probably because of the timidity caused by the persistence of the original inhibition. This makes people afraid that if they become at all interested in these eminently excitable parts, they will suffer from untimely and uncontrollable physical reactions. And that is why, generally speaking, attention is paid to the sex organs only after a long struggle. Even after the establishment of sexual relations with a partner, when people may be strong enough and sufficiently in control of their thoughts and emotions to consider their genital organs, it is rare for them to be able to do so without emotion, and to see these organs merely as either biological necessities or a source of pleasure. What usually happens is that they examine them furtively and that their attitude is loaded with meanings derived from the unconscious, so that the organs become both precious and dangerous, the seat both of pleasure and of the severest prohibitions.

Crude graffiti, *double-entendre* verse and pictures produced by a disordered imagination—all bear witness to the dramatic symbolism invested in both male and female genital organs. The male organ sometimes takes the form of a snake, a rat, an arrow, a sword, and sometimes that of a doll, a bird or an amusing but fickle sprite. The female organs are often represented by a circle with its twin meaning of rest and imprisonment, and while men picture the female organs as a delightful dew-covered meadow, for women they are often more like a wound. If you read St.

John Perse's poem "Etroits sont les Vaisseaux," in his volume entitled *Amers*—perhaps the greatest epic of physical love ever written—you will find most of the images attaching to the male and female sex organs.

Both men and women examine their own bodies in the hope of interpreting them. They shift their gaze rather timidly from the most ordinary parts toward the one concerned with the reproduction of life, and see it through a threefold veil of desire for pleasure, feelings of hostility, and fear. More than any other part of the body, the copulative organ is viewed in the light of the continuous flashes from the opposing poles of the unconscious. Whether this light is sinister or mellow, moonlight or sunlight, it adds new interest to the organ, thus enhancing its physiological virtues and providing pleasure which for the most part doubtless arises from the unconscious itself.

Narcissism may be a subtle exploitation of a person's own body to promote self-expression, but it is also the first step by which sexuality, after withdrawing from the real world in the face of the dangers it presents, cautiously makes its reentry after undergoing a thorough refurbishing. It is the earliest appearance of the unconscious and the preconscious in physical form, and so represents a very tentative return of sexual behavior to the real world.

V

HOMOSEXUAL ATTRACTION AND HETEROSEXUAL FEARS

Moralists and philosophers have reiterated time and again that man is a social animal, naturally adapted to group life. In so doing they have often been misunderstood to mean that establishing contact between one human and another is a simple matter, requiring no more than ordinary spontaneity. This is an illusion soon lost by anyone whose task it is to look after other people; such a one will find himself receiving the confidence of a large number of sad solitaries, timid people who find difficulty in producing the right words and gestures for making contact. Certainly, there are many people of whom it is fair to say that they find normal contact with the opposite sex difficult. Spontaneous sexual contacts can, of course, be observed in the animal world between creatures of the same species living freely in nature, although even there, there are loners and timid individuals. So far as human beings are con-

cerned, however, they have so often had to put the brake
on their instinctual impulses that truly natural behavior
becomes difficult. In matters of sex, genuinely instinctive
relations are not only prohibited, they are, psychologically
speaking, impossible. Prostitution gives a few people the
chance of having relationships that approximate the instinctive, but they deny their own humanity in the very act.

As for spontaneity, it would be more reasonable to expect human beings to remain self-centered and bogged
down in their solitary perverse sexuality. Since this is in
fact not the normal state of affairs, we should inquire what
causes them to come out of their corners.

We should always remember that the unconscious acts
as a screen between individuals. It is all very well to say
that, fundamentally, one individual is very much like another, but this is only the attitude of experts, like clinical
psychologists, and the people being observed do not believe
it. It is only after a great deal of experience, with many
successes and failures along the way, that their eyes open
enough to see what others are really like, and that their
minds perceive how similar indeed people are. In the early
stages people are inclined to believe that their own inmost
thoughts and secret desires are so extraordinary, so out-
standingly absurd or wicked as to be unique, and they hesitate to come out of their shells. They can hardly imagine
that the strange ideas that well up in them, or the sadistic
or masochistic impulses that seize hold of them, have ever
occurred or could possibly occur to the people they esteem
most highly. Depressives are astonished and relieved when
they learn that fairly large numbers of respectable citizens
have been tempted to commit suicide. Similarly, a sexually
shy male may make a discovery that is both sensational and
comforting to him when he observes that the virtuous
young woman of his dreams has the same sort of physical
desire for him as he has for her. We can thus see how great

is the gap that separates us from other people before we start communicating with them, simply because we are usually unaware that our dreams and fears have a great deal in common with theirs.

This is only one case in which a natural obstacle may turn to positive advantage. For, as we have seen, the unconscious uses its imaginary productions to throw up a screen between individuals. But the mere fact of giving expression to the unconscious will bring two people together and offer them satisfactions they would never have known without this detour or delay.

But we should be careful not to give an oversimplified answer to the question of how this comes about. If we are dealing with people who are outgoing and by nature not very egocentric, it is easy to see how contact is made. Not only will their unconscious express itself freely in words, gestures and attitudes; in addition none of the individuals concerned will have much trouble in paying attention to what the others are expressing. Yet we must try to explain what is involved in paying attention in this way.

For human beings are separated by so many psychological barriers that to come together and meet each other, they have to do far more than merely express themselves, each one separately. To use an analogy, in a play it sometimes happens that there is no real contact between the actors, so that while each of them plays his part strictly in accordance with the instructions of the director, there is no coherence other than that imposed by the director himself from outside. Critics would say that the cast cannot act. But at the point when it is only just emerging from domination by the unconscious, is humanity very different from a troupe of bad actors paying no attention to one another? Is it unfair to feel that, taken by and large, groups of human beings consist of individuals who do no more than perform parts allotted by custom, convention or law? Similarly, is it unreasonable to describe a good many couples as a fortuitous combination of two actors, one taking the part of the husband and father, the other of the wife and mother, who fail to pick up each other's cues, as if the only thing that mattered was the strict observance of the rules fixed by the Great Producer, be he Law, Nature, Society or God? With such a rigid outlook, so far removed from the richness that can be achieved through free expression on both sides, it is no wonder that couples fall apart and find themselves compelled to recognize that their union did not bring the happiness they had hoped for.

1

Attention to other people, one of the prerequisites for genuine contact, grows out of the ambitions connected with narcissism. I would like to demonstrate this, first by giving examples and then by attempting a more theoretical analysis.

As long as girls have no sexual needs, they tend not to bother about dress. Their taste in clothing is straightforward, natural and unaffected. But as soon as they begin to take notice of sexual stimuli, they stop being so easy to satisfy. Pulled now this way, now that, they find much more difficulty in choosing. They want unusual clothes that project an image of their changing and violently emotional selves. At this stage mothers have to interfere to make sure that ordinary, respectable garments are worn when appropriate. There is no doubt that anxiety makes mothers less tactful than they might be, and they would often do better to wait for time to take its course. For if girls are allowed a certain amount of liberty, they will fairly soon adopt a reasonable enough style both in their behavior and in their dress. But how are they to find this

personal style except by carefully observing the behavior
and mannerisms of those of their friends who seem to have
the best taste and the best chance of being attractive? What
better way is there of "becoming oneself" than watching
and imitating others, taking what seems best and leaving
the rest? Not only is this finding oneself the mainspring of
all honest rivalry, it is also first and foremost the stimulus
par excellence for taking an interest in others.

This is the point at which objectivity and subjectivity
meet, where observation of others coincides with a desire
to be oneself. To work from the particular to the general,
let us analyze the data available to us. I shall start by ask-
ing a question about a typical girl: Do you think that she
is altogether aware of her desire to please throughout the
whole period that she is closely observing her companions'
style? Most assuredly she is not, at any rate not at the beginning; she will not become aware of it until much later,
even though the desire itself is actively present from the
very moment that she begins to consider others as rivals.
It is the first active factor to be seen by outside observers
and the last to be noticed by the person herself. The girl's
perceptions move back and forth between her friends' appearance and her own, making continual comparisons. The
only purpose of her glances at others is to enable her to
consider her own image, while her glances at herself serve
only as a basis of comparison with others. Instead of con-
templating herself in a mirror, she is comparing two separate people in a single reflection.

For this comparison to be of any use, it must bring to
light the other person's qualities and the observer's defects. If it were to have the opposite result, i.e., revealing
the other person's defects and the observer's qualities, the
comparison would be a waste of effort and would only represent an attempt by the unconscious to compensate for
feelings of inferiority or to remove the traces of some sup-

posed injury. But we are now dealing with matters outside the field of unconscious overcompensation, since a genuine personality is now coming into existence. Unwittingly guided by her desire to please, the girl is comparing the two images only in order to bring hers more closely into line with that of the person she admires.

As she wishes to enhance her powers of seduction, she will devote time to considering the good qualities in her own image only in order to help her become more like her model. Theoretically, she will analyze the model in great detail in order to discover its outstanding qualities, while in her own image she will look for all the more repulsive features and try to get rid of them. To put it in still another way, she will make every effort to break out of her neutrality and insignificance and to acquire a character of her own. And for this purpose she will base herself on an outside model.

It is of course obvious that in order to be of any use, the model must be neither too different—otherwise, he or she would have no narcissistic value and would be no help as somebody to copy—nor too similar, for then copying him or her would not achieve any improvement. Nobody can serve as a model to be copied unless he or she is both similar and different. In addition, he or she must appeal to the onlooker as embodying something within reach, that is to say, as someone whom the onlooker might become by emphasizing certain features, and a visible, living demonstration of what she could achieve by making the best of the qualities with which she has been endowed by nature. It is only thus that a model can be an encouragement and a consolation, and someone worth loving. One of the reasons girls are so fascinated by female film stars is that they console the youngsters for being as they are by showing them what they could become with a little effort.

Rivalry is thus composed of three separate elements: *(a)*

underlying every effort at self-improvement, barely conscious but very much alive and carrying with it the earliest sex drive, there is the desire to be noticed, to excite and attract others; (b) there is the more or less deliberate intention to use the greatest possible number of mental and physical attributes toward that end; and (c) to enhance the erotic attraction of both body and mind, there is the detailed comparison with people considered more expert at exciting others—people who are neither too similar nor too different from the observer. I shall discuss each of these elements separately:

a. The desire to please is the outward manifestation of the sexual excitement which was the starting point for this part of our inquiry. We have agreed to define sexual behavior as the whole series of actions and reactions by which two beings come together and try to stimulate each other by mutual touch. These actions have so far been held in check, giving rise to sexual manifestations by the unconscious which have, however, superseded neither the state of organic excitement nor the instinctive tendencies. At the first favorable opportunity, and seizing on any psychic factor which can be given sexual significance, the inhibited impulse will break out, and set off the series of actions that are defined as sexual behavior. Although held in check and partly suppressed, the original sexual excitement survives through a whole series of manifestations by the unconscious and preconscious, and gives these an erotic significance at the moment of their emergence into the real world. This is the way in which the expressive elements of the personality are formed, and they have two separate functions: the first is to give external shape and form to inner conflicts; the second, to stimulate the onlookers attracted by this exteriorization of unconscious sexuality.

b. It is perhaps worth pointing out once again that this exteriorization of the unconscious reflects its contradictory features and explains why the characteristics that people wish to emphasize in their narcissistic phase are neither isolated nor homogenous. It is not simply a question of making the skin smoother, the eyes brighter or speech bolder; only rather simple souls expect to increase their seductiveness merely by emphasizing their naturally attractive physical attributes. Most often, the aim is to make not only physical details (features, figure, walk) but also words and ideas more expressive. The overall result should be an expression, either simultaneous or successive, of the light and shade, the gentleness and strength of the psyche. Insofar as speech is concerned, only the most naive lover could imagine that it should only reflect a uniform and homogeneous soul. To avoid monotony, which is the worst enemy of happy love, it should express a range of intense feelings, as varied as the many facets of the unconscious itself. A lover has the best chance of winning his or her beloved if he avoids speaking too bluntly. The more his words stylize the fears, desires and ambitions of the unconscious without thrusting them too violently into the real world, the more will the loved one like them, find her own desires reflected in them and wish to hear more. I once knew a man who started his love affairs by describing the joys and woes of his past life. This made him seem like a predestined conqueror, and the ladies only admired him the more.

Sartre feels that the metaphysical conversations which provide timid lovers with a screen behind which to hold hands and let themselves be caught in the snare of sensuality are all examples of deliberate bad faith. I do not take such a harsh view, first because I do not feel as he does about the flesh being a snare, and second—and far more important—because it is the nature of human beings to pass through a phase in which they must reveal their inner feelings before achieving a state of mutual goodwill, and it is this demonstration of feeling which makes such conversations both awkwardly metaphysical and moving.

If it is to remain human, sexuality must pass through the cauldron of the emotions and take on their hue. This is well understood by people who try to make their bodies and minds not only more exciting but also more expressive of the fundamental emotions of fear, anxiety, sadness, anger, pride and joy. I should add that it is not really a matter of becoming bogged down in emotion, but of expressing and stylizing it.

c. Finally, human beings pay such great attention to those who attract them, that is, to those who seem to reflect the strongest expression of their own personality and sexuality, mainly because they wish to increase their own expressiveness. As they are concerned with upgrading all the abilities enabling them to "put themselves over" to others, it is only natural for them to be attracted by those who have the most similar characteristics, so that the other person's features and conduct tune in with the deeper feelings which they themselves have not yet succeeded in stylizing.

That is why we begin to understand ourselves only by looking in the mirror held up for us by those whom we admire. Let me say in passing that this is the basis of all the projection tests used in clinical psychology. Human beings start expressing themselves by admiring some people and spurning others. All of us seem to have a sort of psychic perceptiveness which enables us to detect in others the essential aspects of our own inner selves. Once we discover individuals who have the same "form" and "tone" as ourselves, we love them in a way that could be described as "not disinterested," to say the least. We worship them like adolescents, in the hope of learning what makes them tick. For example, a young writer does not want merely to assimilate the ideas or metaphors of the master he is following, which would be unprofitable plagiarism; he wants to absorb the tautness, balance and rhythm of his style. The young man's aim is to capture the drive that makes the master speak and write, dictates his choice of words and images, and inspires his works as a whole. A young writer's destiny is cast at the moment when he chooses his models. Proust was already Proust when he started devouring Saint-Simon's *Mémoires* and Balzac's *Comédie humaine*.

To turn to some less distinguished examples and to return to sexuality, the first way in which a young woman expresses herself is to choose an adult woman to copy. Will she be a gentle, maternal person whose rounded shape suggests warm protectiveness, an Amazon of whom it is difficult to say whether she is more male or female, or a perfectly formed Venus more concerned just now with beauty than maternity, but ready for motherhood one day soon? It is not without significance that we can think up a behavior pattern, a way of life or even a whole career for any woman, whether she is real, or whether we merely see her depicted in stone or described on the printed page. For this is what external expression either through the body or the personality really means. It is to achieve this sort of self-expression that young women start their conscious emotional existence by attaching themselves to someone, whether real or imaginary, of the same sex; they are trying to capture the model's potentialities and mold these to their own needs.

2

We should now be in a position to understand why persons of the same sex are attracted to one another. The attraction is usually generated by someone whom we both admire and envy, who stands for many of the things that we would like to be, and who also possesses the erotic quality we would like to have ourselves. People who have a homosexual experience go further, and bring into play all the nervous and physiological sides of their sexuality to express their admiration. It is as if, hoist with their own petard, they forget that they are trying to find themselves in someone else of the same sex, or as if in order to find out how to influence members of the opposite sex and discover what is likely to impress them, they think it desirable to play the part themselves. In brief, we may say that before passing favorable judgment on the sexual attractiveness of their own bodies and organs, people examine them in other individuals who are as like them as possible, and this implies being of the same sex. They try out the effectiveness of a given display of manliness or femininity by standing in for a woman or a man. Making use of their imagination, they hope that physical relations with those they consider models of manliness or femininity will, by a process of osmosis, lead to identification or an exchange of personalities and characteristics which will turn them into accomplished men and women. What is sad is that the pleasure thus enjoyed tends to make the participants think that they have in fact something in common with the opposite sex. What started more or less as a game of trying on an identity turns into real life, with people trying to find a real identity. The tormented nature of most of the homosexual relationships I have had the opportunity of analyzing has arisen from the fact that, paradoxically, each of the partners was trying to augment the characteristic features of his own sex by identifying himself with the opposite sex. I am sure that my readers will agree that this is a difficult and unprofitable situation.

Although these homosexual affairs are often entered into by disparate partners—an old person and a young one, a man of culture and a boor—this should not lead us wrongly to believe that there is any real imitation of heterosexuality, with one person playing an active virile role and the other a passive feminine one. That would be an oversimplified view of the situation, which can only arise from considering in a heterosexual light a relationship in which the difference between the sexes in fact plays little part. We should also beware of the specious arguments by which homosexuals themselves later justify their behavior and try to make it seem similar to heterosexual relations. When a man of culture seeks pleasure with an ill-mannered tough, it is easy to say that as he considers himself to be like a woman, it is only natural that he should seek pleasure with someone having the most obvious attributes of manliness. My own feeling, however, is that the identification with the opposite sex is often secondary and more of a justification than anything else. The reason that the boor is so interesting to the man of culture in the first place is that the tough exterior incorporates in obvious and visible form the cultured man's secret dream of being powerful and strong.

At a deeper level, the image of a strong man embracing a weak one so well expresses the inner conflict between violence and gentleness that torments the cultured man that it becomes both attractive and erotic, and he will not be content until he has turned the image into a real act. Everything that comes later—e.g., imitation of heterosexual relations, transvestism, and so forth—will be only a form of blowup intended for public consumption. The pleasure derived from turning the image into reality will only increase the tendency to abnormal behavior.

This analysis of homosexual attraction, which is based on the erotic effect of any act of self-expression by other people, especially if they are of the same sex as the onlooker, naturally does not cover all homosexual behavior. It is, for example, well known that this sort of behavior is not peculiar to human beings but is found throughout the animal world. How is this to be explained except as the result of mistakes by nature in the course of its experiments, absence of suitable partners, or the presence of a dominant male who captures all the females, leaving only substitute pleasures for the weak? There is no doubt whatever that many forms of abnormal human behavior can be attributed to this type of situation, and yet I believe that such explanations are valid only for simpletons suffering from arrested development, or for people who are cut off from the opposite sex by *force majeure,* as in a prison camp. In these circumstances, the endogenous result of sexual needs is to give each sex stimulant (voice, skin, bearing) a significance of its own, completely hiding the personality of the individuals to whom it belongs.

We know that there are both various forms of homosexual behavior and different levels of homosexuality. Of course, it would be wrong to exclude physiological factors a priori, although research in this connection has so far scarcely produced any useful results. But I will restrict myself to discussing the role of homosexual *attraction* in the life of normal human beings. This type of attraction is specifically human, and far from being a deficiency or representing disequilibrium, it implies a certain superiority to mere animal sexuality, representing, as it does, a transition from the narcissism mentioned above to heterosexual attraction. Homosexual attraction becomes abnormal only when it is exaggerated and the person concerned cannot use it is a stepping stone toward higher forms of sexual conduct.

Homosexual attraction is the manifestation of the attractiveness exerted by our ideal image of ourselves when we see it reflected in someone else. Our pleasure at the sight of someone whose behavior, gestures and style of life truly express one aspect or another of our own conflicts, while of an artistic nature, actually verges on the sexual in that it may at any moment spread through the body and activate those processes which trigger sexual behavior in the narrow sense.

In explaining homosexual attraction, psychoanalysts fall back on the compensatory identification formula, meaning that young men identify themselves with their mothers, and girls with their fathers. They also lay emphasis on the bisexual nature of every being, male and female. All this may very well be true, but many of these explanations seem to me very superficial. I shall start with identification with the opposite sex, meaning that a boy behaves like a girl. On the one hand, this oversimplified description hardly ever really fits the case. Sometimes, as the people concerned are unable to describe what is happening to them, they accept this facile explanation just to make the observer happy. On the other hand, people who are better able to express themselves usually reject such interpretations and reveal glimpses of reactions that are far more complex than a straightforward identification with someone from their childhood. While it is true that they do in fact often identify themselves in some such way, this would seem to be rather effect than cause, that is to say, an imaginary construction arising out of the attraction exercised by the partner's style on the diffuse unconscious of the person involved.

If proof is required of this explanation, I shall start by taking shelter behind the authority of experts such as Plato and Freud. While it is true that authority has no real weight in science, it would be presumptuous to wish to rediscover everything anew and to disdain the work of men who have penetrated further into the maze of human motives than anyone else without using dubious quantitative methods. No discussion of homosexuality can ignore the description given in Plato's famous dialogue on love in the *Symposium*. The attraction exercised by the ideal, that is to say in psychological terms, by the inner projection of the conflict between our aspirations and our limitations, plays a major role. Freud's explanation is similar, for in his succinct but thorough study of narcissism, he compares certain homosexual choices to love of self (narcissistic investment, *Ichbesetzung* in German).

I would like to cite in support of this view an accepted opinion which, while it has no indisputable scientific authority, does at least express an implicit understanding of homosexual attraction. In the popular view, both in our society and in more primitive ones, homosexuality is particularly prevalent in the artistic world. Statistics do not support this view; on the contrary, they show that this type of behavior occurs in the same proportions in all professional groupings. But even so, the popular view is not necessarily altogether wrong, for it may be correct in linking the artistic temperament with intense homosexual attraction, although it is certainly mistaken in its attitude to outward appearances and in seeing artistic temperaments only in the world of professional artists. When delving into the field of psychological forces, it is dangerous to let oneself be led astray by outward appearances. The fact that apparent toughs are homosexuals does not invalidate my thesis, for coarse physical features and crudely vulgar actions may conceal a sensitive mind that is responsive to the styles of people and things. The tough also has an unconscious, and he, too, is torn between his aspirations toward improvement and the knowledge of his limitations, between desire and prohibition. And so he can be attracted by people more refined than himself who incarnate everything he would like to be and everything that he cannot be. Sensitivity to other people's style is the prerogative of no class and no profession; it is a purely individual matter, and it depends entirely on the intensity of the unconscious emotions.

A rather ordinary observation will provide additional

confirmation. This is that men generally tend to compare the erotic attractiveness of their rivals with their own, not on the basis of the number of the rivals' adventures or their successes with the opposite sex, but on the basis of their effect on themselves. An individual possessing nothing more than crude sexual instincts would not take this round-about course; he would make a headlong rush toward the most attractive mate, thrusting aside any rivals with all the strength or wiles at his command. He would be quite un-able to adopt a reflective attitude involving self-criticism to see whether he has the desired qualities. Once he had been attracted by a woman he would have no awareness of the erotic qualities of his neighbor and could certainly not talk about them. That he does in fact talk about them and compare himself with others proves that his relationships are not merely a matter of instinct or internal trigger mechanisms, but rather consist of a system of externally per-ceived data related to another system of internal uncon-scious elements. It is, of course, this sudden, exciting con-cordance of the style of a person or thing with the pattern of the unconscious that arouses artistic pleasure and gives all our passions their powerful, almost obligatory nature. Homosexual attraction is one of the forms of this sort of pleasure. It arises from an abrupt encounter with some-one whose physical and mental makeup give visible, living expression to the predominant desires of the unconscious. A man who has not yet plucked up the courage to *behave* like a man will be attracted toward people who incarnate his own idea of manliness. This idea will of course vary from person to person and place to place, but in our West-ern society it is often an image of strength triumphant over all obstacles and every form of resistance. Similarly, women are attracted to others whose style coincides with their idea of femininity, and while the image has also varied with individuals and cultures, for many years the general one in the West was that of a gentle, embracing personality whose inner fears all had fled.

The errors people make in assessing the erotic attraction of others of the same sex serve only to highlight the narcissistic nature of homosexual attraction and its foundations in the properties of the unconscious. Those considered most attractive by members of their own sex often have far less success with the opposite sex. This failure in objective appreciation proves that homosexual attraction takes place in the subjective unconscious, and that it arises from a similarity of nature between a person with a particular style and the imaginary world of the onlooker which is directed to certain special forms of expression. This similarity of nature was well observed by Jung. His only mistake was to oversimplify the situation and to define the unconscious in an unnecessarily narrow fashion, as if it were necessarily male when the person in the outside world is female, and vice versa. In practice, if we wish to understand how attractions between individuals arise, we should avoid making any clear-cut distinction between males and females. When emotions are first aroused in us by other people, we do not yet have any clear perception of the difference between male and female, and we are not yet really either masculine or feminine. We are only an organism experiencing erotic thrills and suffering from violent conflicts in its unconscious. The first people to be at all attractive will be those whose characteristics and behavior seem most likely to offer a solution to the problems which are paralyzing us. In most cases these will be people of the same sex, but no clear idea of masculinity or femininity will enter into the matter at this stage. What underlies these early attractions is our effort to clarify our image of ourselves in one way or another.

3

The range of conflicts in the unconscious is so great that it would be unwise to state categorically that the earliest attractions will necessarily be homosexual. It would be more accurate to say that at this stage people are not very greatly concerned with the differences between male and female. What is important is the similarity between the style of the other person and the content of the unconscious of the attracted party. It may work out that the very first encounter will be between people of opposite sex but similar emotional style. But if the attraction appears heterosexual, this is pure chance. On the psychological side it would still be correct to speak of homosexuality or at least of a diversion of narcissistic love.

But in psychology chance must not be considered a factor. At least in our own complex society where members of the two sexes are often educated by different methods and in separate institutions, we must expect to see the earliest attraction develop between people of the same sex. While the social environment certainly has an influence, there is another, more personal factor. It is certain that, regardless of the form of society in which people live, differences of anatomy—which are so extraordinary to a child—of clothing and of behavior together produce such a wide separation between the sexes that it is difficult in the early stages for emotional harmony to grow up between them. And so we may say that in general attraction is likely to be felt first between people of similar outward appearance.

In normal circumstances, the opposite sex starts by being frightening before it becomes attractive. Sexual differences in the organs, the general bearing of the body, the voice and other secondary characteristics do not of course deter members of the animal world, since their instincts operate in the way appropriate to the species. In human beings, on the contrary, these differences are assessed by the unconscious as a danger and an impediment. Strictly speaking, at this point we ought to offer a general outline of the psychology of human beings when they are faced by something unknown or different in outward appearances from themselves. Animal psychologists can already provide a great deal of information in this connection. Practical experience also shows that everything strange and different is usually felt to be dangerous, and at the same time both fascinating and frightening. Finally, clinical experience shows that the most noticeably different sex organs— a man's penis, a woman's vulva—acquire quite fantastic significance in most people's unconscious, and so make early emotional contact difficult between boy and girl. Moreover, these anatomical differences are made more significant and frightening by the great number of taboos with which they are surrounded. But even without the taboos, there are plenty of visible differences which confirm the belief, rooted in the unconscious, that there are two opposing masculine and feminine worlds with quite different aims, each ready to defend itself from attack by the other. Who would dare affirm that he has never looked at a member of the opposite sex with mistrust? Is there any society in the world where intercourse between the sexes takes place free of tension? Even the gentlest, most peaceful societies provide examples of the hidden struggle between men and women. They may do all they can to make men and women legally equal, sharing the same work and having the same habits, but there are still dances and jokes inspired by the remnants of hostility toward the opposite sex. There is a general rule which says that whenever human beings find the slightest differences, they will magnify them and turn them into dangers, even though biologically speaking the differences are really complementary and entirely natural.

It is against this background of latent hostility that individuals read fantastic meanings into anatomical differences. Boys see their penis as a weapon giving them strength and a girl's sex organ as a point of weakness. Laymen are often amazed at the importance accorded by psychoanalysts to the fact that girls suffer from feelings of inferiority because they have no penis, while boys enjoy a secret pride because they have one. While this analysis may well seem childish, it accurately interprets the ideas of many children who are reduced to interpreting everything in terms of force, that is, in terms of possession and defense. But adults retain their childish ideas in the back of their mind, and the same ideas exist in diffuse but nonetheless permanent form in the customs and habits of the societies in which they live. If you listen to people making jokes you will soon hear their childhood symbols coming to the surface. The penis is turned into an arrow, a sword or a dangerous weapon which gives them cause either for pride, or for sorrow because it has not been used enough. A woman's genitalia are transformed into an opening protected by a portcullis or a dangerous cavern. Coitus is made to seem like a struggle in which each of the two parties tries to vanquish the other with his or her own weapons. I would go so far as to say that scientific writings on the psychological differences between men and women, where men are said to be aggressive and women defensive, are affected by these fantasies which picture the sex organs as dangerous instruments and which are themselves the result of fear of the opposite sex.

Fear is the main source of our mistaken ideas. At night, the trees of the forest turn into ghosts. But they at least are inanimate objects which know nothing of our fears and are quite unaware of the identity so falsely conferred on them. Things become more complicated when the fear is attached to a man or a woman. For, the person who is feared is almost bound to react either by fear on his own part, or by annoyance or aggression; only rarely will he or she react by trying to calm our fears. It would be most useful, especially for psychologists of sex, if a study could be made of the mutual reactions induced by fear. We should no doubt find that the person who is feared is forced unwillingly to face up to his own suppressed aggressiveness (otherwise, why should anyone be afraid of him?) and that he will be very annoyed to have his bad temper, which he has worked hard to keep hidden, thus revealed. We should then be able to understand the paradox that people who are afraid make others aggressive, and that weak people call down upon themselves the harshness of others.

Fear is not only a bad counsellor; it is in particular a cause of division. It never leads to closer understanding, at any rate between people of roughly the same age. The only time that fear is met by any effort to help is when a mother sees it in her child. Apart from this the main result of showing fear is to awaken aggressiveness in others. People become frightened when they see fear in someone else, and a slow buildup of tension between two frightened people often leads to an explosion. Relations are often broken off or put on a more distant footing to avoid such an outcome.

Clinical psychologists are often struck by the frequency with which people with no particular aversion to the opposite sex take preventive steps of this sort. From their own account, they seem simply to be shy. Further investigation shows not only that they are lacking in courage, but also that they surreptitiously reject any advances whatsoever. Delving deeper still, it will be found that, contrary to the usual desires of human beings, they wish to keep their distance from the opposite sex in order to avoid the risk of a possibly hostile encounter. I do not mean that these people are not attracted. On the contrary, they long so much for a man or a woman and have such an idealized notion of emotional relationships that they avoid entering into real relations with a partner of their own, for fear of being disappointed and being unable to bear up under the impact of an aggressive attitude which would compel them to abandon any hope of achieving their ideal or assuaging their longing. Sometimes, although they have no personal experience of the problems of life together, they have some foreboding of them. Even though they may be unable to explain why they are afraid of closer intimacy, they have an unconscious ability to see ahead, and so they ward off any event that might lead to a permanent union, which they realize in some obscure way would be very tempestuous. All these forebodings, I hasten to add, are only the fruit of early fears. I do not mean that anyone actually believes that members of the other sex are deliberately hostile, but that being afraid themselves, they are anxious about the effects of their fear on a potential partner. In other words, they anticipate the disagreeable explosions that would occur as the only means of dissipating the tensions born of their joint fears.

The sources of this mutually induced fear have now been identified. I mentioned one of them earlier when explaining how human beings are afraid of anything that is different, or can be described as strange or unusual. Since of course the object with which anyone is most familiar is his own body, complete with its own special features, both visible and hidden, we may be reasonably sure that the first time we see a body that is different from ours, we shall be both surprised and somewhat afraid. The result is likely to be so upsetting that we turn things upside down in our minds, so that the male organ of love seems to be an offensive weapon and the female organ a wound. It is to Freud that we owe our present understanding of the influence of anatomical differences on the formation of male and female ways of thought. But as the founder of psychoanalysis usually restricted himself to explaining the difficulties of adults by reference to the misconceptions and conflicts of their childhood, we may well wonder whether he was not rather hasty in leaving adult psychology on one side. Anatomical differences seem striking only to comparatively young children; adults, in the biological sense, do not need to be particularly intelligent to understand their real significance. And yet, their timidity when faced by members of the opposite sex continues even after they have reached a proper understanding. If someone continues to construe these differences in an irrational way throughout adolescence or even into maturity he is not altogether free from disingenuousness; for he is using his fantasies to express his deep animosity to the opposite sex in symbolic form. At this stage the bodily differences between males and females are not a genuine cause of fear, but are exploited for purposes of expression—I would even go so far as to say for poetic purposes—as the image of the conflict between love and hate. The sex organs thus become the focus of all the unreal and ambiguous feelings toward the opposite sex. We should therefore look deeper for the causes of mutual fear between members of the two sexes.

It cannot really be claimed that the emotions experienced by children when they discover the differences between one body and another are a sufficient cause in themselves, for these emotions vanish, but the fears remain. But a great deal occurs between the discovery of bodily differences and the full development of the sex organs, and it would be wrong to ignore these changes. And even after the system has become fully awake to erotic stimuli, individuals undergo a great deal of internal development. It would therefore seem reasonable to seek in the *unconscious* for some explanation of the mutual fears of members of the opposite sexes.

The unconscious does not spew forth imaginary ideas at random. All its creations start from emotional disturbances in people who are being pulled this way and that by tenderness and ferocity, pleasure and duty, rebellion and submission, and their purpose is to find a point of balance. Every sort of tendency is expressed in the form of images borrowed from reality in which the person concerned is intimately involved. But if all these different images were to be adopted with equal favor the result would only be confusion. Some must be rejected as soon as they appear, while others must be given a sympathetic welcome and fostered in order to counteract the rejected ones. This is only an application of the equilibrium principle. All the possible images of the self are sketched in broad outline, but they do not retain the same status for long, since some are directly contrary to others. Contrasts begin to form, since accepting one identification means rejecting an opposing one. An individual's instinctive ambivalence is satisfied in this way, since every possible person he could become appears in one form or another; but in a sense, too, it becomes irrelevant, since a spontaneous choice is made by which the individual considers certain images of himself as favorable and others unfavorable.

In order to grasp the reasons for fear of the opposite sex, it is essential to have a thorough understanding of this closely balanced game of identification and counteridentification. Before going on to illustrate the connection between the two, I shall therefore give a few clinical examples of identification and counteridentification.

My first is that of a young man whose chief desire is to be energetic to the point of violence. He utterly rejects any tendency in him to be gentle, weak or yielding. We might well be tempted to say that he is a model of masculinity. In fact, he hardly qualifies for that description, and the word "masculinity" is both too restrictive and too vague to encompass his desires. What he is really trying to do is to bring together in his own person all the tendencies connected with the idea of struggle, and what is important to understand is that his conscious positive identification with people representing strength and struggle covers a counteridentification with people representing gentleness. Preference for anything always implies repugnance for its opposite, and emphasis on one aspect of oneself can be achieved only by denying another.

To take a second example, let us look at the case of a girl who has chosen rebellion and pleasure. This does not in the least mean that she has given herself over to a life of debauchery. We are dealing with the world of the imagination, and the choice she makes is only one way of saying something forcefully. But this emphasis on the venturesome and nonconforming side of her nature must necessarily involve a denigration of all forms of submissiveness, which also enter into her character. This girl would be revolted by anyone who reflected the part of herself that she does not wish to be at any price.

These two examples are obvious enough for us to move on to the problem of fear of the other sex. It is reasonable to start by saying that everyone is likely to attribute to the people least like themselves, i.e., members of the opposite sex, the features of the image of themselves which they refuse to bring into existence and to which they attach what I have called a counteridentification, or negative identification. The Greeks attributed to the barbarians all the coarse vices which they wished to deny they practiced themselves. Men whose ideal is one of action attribute to women the taste for idleness and relaxation which is actually part of their own nature, but which their ideal compels them to forego. I have often noticed that it is the most chaste people—chaste in the sense that they would never forgive themselves for any sexual thoughts—who are the most likely to speak of members of the opposite sex as being ready for any sort of debauchery. They see in individuals who are as unlike them as possible, both physically and morally, all the characteristics that they do not wish to have themselves. It is an inescapable law of nature that anything that is too violently denied a place in someone's own soul will seem to be found in equally exaggerated form in those who are least like them in physical appearance. It is also a very disturbing law because it makes many people very annoyed when they find themselves unjustly accused of having characteristics or desires which they either do not have at all, or perhaps only in a very embryonic form, just like anyone else. If we were perfectionists, should we not be upset to discover that we are very rarely taken for what we are—a mixture of rather contradictory desires and features—but that we are considered to be everything that others do not wish to be, in fact the embodiment of their forbidden desires?

My readers will have recognized the last few lines as a description of the *projection* mechanism. Jung and Szondi devoted special attention to it, and believed that it was the basis for an explanation of how people choose their mates. According to both Jung and Szondi, we select as our partner the member of the opposite sex who presents most visibly (or phenotypically) those features or characteristics which are hidden, repressed or recessive in ourselves and which are innate, if unconscious, components of our very being (or, in other words, are our genotypical selves). Where these two authors go wrong, in my view, is in the rigid distinction they make between dominant and recessive characteristics. For example, the line they draw between *animus,* said by them to be a masculine term designating all the conscious traits of the personality, and *anima,* a feminine term covering unconscious and repressed traits, seems to me altogether too black and white. In addition, this distinction implies a conception of both masculinity and femininity that experience shows to be rather mythical or transcendental. Clinical psychologists, who are aware that most people's psyches are far from fully developed, do not believe in masculinity or femininity; they tend to believe that there are only people, trying to find themselves in the dark. In so doing, they make clumsy use of any psychological or literary clichés that may come to hand, and these in turn give rise to images of masculinity or femininity, as the case may be. I would of course be the last to deny that there is a difference between male and female behavior both in the biological field, and if the person concerned is well rounded, in the psychological field as well. But at the level of development we are investigating at this point, we have still not reached the stage of objective concepts, nor yet that of the equilibrium which could take the form of a return to natural simplicity after all the peregrinations through the lands of the imagination and the unconscious. We are still dealing with an area that is close to the unconscious, and we know all the tricks and turns to which the unconscious will resort in order to work its aggressive tendencies out of the system. An individual trying to develop his personality takes as his guideposts a set of identifications and counteridentifications that have very little to do with objective views of masculinity or femininity. Consequently, at the risk of being less systematic than Jung or Szondi, I would say that the distinction should be made between images of the self given favorable appraisal and those given unfavorable appraisal, and that we project onto other people those images we consider unfavorable and of which we wish to rid ourselves in consequence.

I would like to put forward a second criticism of the theory advanced by these two great men. Before using the projection theory to explain why people choose one mate rather than another, they should have used it to explain why the same people are afraid of the most attractive potential partners. For projection gives birth to fear before or certainly no later than it does to attraction. This is not difficult to understand if we bear in mind that it is the negative features of ourselves that we project onto members of the opposite sex. Our fear of the opposite sex is often no more than a reflection of our fear of the banned and rejected part of ourselves. As men see first in the features and behavior of their female acquaintances those characteristics they like least in themselves, they are perhaps really running from themselves when they run away from these women. On the other side of the picture, women are not happy at finding in their men friends the characteristics that they have been fighting in their own soul in order to build what they believe to be the best personality for themselves.

To give an example, an ambitious, bossy woman marries a gentle, modest man without quite understanding why. All their friends imagine that the one will complement the other, and that everything will be fine. Naturally, things do not work out like that at all. After a few months of marriage they begin to criticize each other and—this may at first sight seem surprising—most of the criticism is devoted to the very characteristics that had earlier led them to decide to marry. Thus the wife pours abuse on her husband because he is not manly enough, and while before they were married she found his gentleness attractive, she can now no longer stand it because it makes him seem too effeminate. This is a very serious inconsistency. Many writers would say that the wife did not really know what she wanted; after all, she chose the man for his gentleness and then rejected him because he continued to be gentle in marriage. But is this capriciousness bad faith or simply the operation of the laws governing attraction and repulsion between men and women? What actually happened? If we look into the whole affair more closely, it becomes evident that the husband was not as gentle as might appear; he was a mixture of stubbornness and goodness. His wife had chosen him for his happy nature. But as the days went by, she began to detect certain signs of weakness, to pick out all the passive features of his character, and to take every opportunity of "keeping him in his place." It was just as if she wanted to turn him into a woman. Of course, there was nothing explicit about this, and in fact she was quite unhappy about the bullying way in which she treated him.

To say that her behavior was "castrating" does not explain anything for us, nor does it help her. What is more important is to bring to light the unconscious mechanism behind her projection. It might be described something like this: as she was ambitious, hardworking and bossy (at least that is the image of herself that she was trying to establish), she had to repress the complementary characteristics of submissiveness, relaxation and tranquillity. Now, it was of course just those features that she discovered in her husband, and which made him quite unbearable for her. At the beginning of their life together she unconsciously transferred to him everything she did not wish to be, and his defects—for who has none?—were intensified as a result. Then, she began consciously to be irritated by the negative image of herself that she had succeeded in fastening on her husband.

The propinquity of life together makes us model our spouse on the worst and least-conscious image of ourselves, without our knowing it. And then we are surprised to find that we cannot stand a partner who is made up of the bits and pieces that we did not wish to have anything to do with for ourselves.

4

It is by studying these projection phenomena that we shall learn how to be less afraid of members of the opposite sex and to enjoy their natural attractions more easily. The less we project negative or disliked images onto them, the less shall we feel the need for a defensive attitude toward them. And is not the best way of reducing the number of images thus projected to diminish the need for blinding ourselves to our real selves?

A person who is no longer afraid of seeing himself with all his desires, however contradictory, and is prepared to accept their existence within him behind the facade of his public personality, without worrying about being led away by them into actions he would later want to disavow, is likely to find relations with others very easy. He is not upset by finding in them characteristics that had previously disturbed him because they were too much like the forbidden traits in his own nature; these are now mere resemblances or similarities giving no cause for alarm. As most of our withdrawals from contact with others arise from withdrawal from a part of our own selves, it is natural that conversely a broader knowledge of ourselves and a calmer acceptance of what we find there will help us to be more tolerant of the defects we find in others. In any event, we shall cease to blow them up out of all real proportion. Really extraordinary changes can occur in a relationship when one partner understands that the negative image, which he or she had unconsciously been transferring to the other, is his or her own.

I am reminded of the true story of a husband who could not bear the slightest sign of laziness in his wife. He himself got up late in the morning, but he became very bad tempered when his wife, from time to time, decided to stay in bed with him on a Sunday morning, or to take her breakfast in bed. During the day the husband ran about a great deal and gave himself the impression that he was doing a lot of work. At the same time, when his wife complained that she had too much to cope with he would tell her she was being feeble, boast of how much he had to do, and start a tirade against women in general, complaining that they had difficult characters and were congenital complainers. At last one day he suddenly realized that he wasn't really doing very much, and that he did not like what he was doing. A few successes in business at the right moment encouraged him to continue. He started getting up earlier in the morning. Do you suppose that he became more demanding with his wife? Now that he was really in a position to set himself up as an example, he took good care not to do so. He was more lenient with her when she took time to rest, and began to encourage her to stay in bed and relax. His wife's image was in fact no longer overlaid with the weakness which he had earlier tried to transfer from himself to her.

So far as sex is concerned, the change from homosexual attraction to heterosexual attraction requires a transformation of this sort. The image of a member of the opposite sex is always overlaid with a large number of features which do not really belong there, for they are really our own which we have rejected. For that image to become objective and as attractive as it might be, the overlays must be removed. The most beautiful woman in the world will leave a man cold, or at least hesitant, if he is in the habit of discharging the vices, weaknesses or tendencies of which he wishes to rid himself, on the opposite sex. She will be able to exercise her real charm on him only when the projected characteristics have been erased, and her true self can appear without causing alarm. Generally speaking, a woman can be herself, that is, she can allow herself to express her real inner conflicts and follow her own nature, only with a man who is no longer afraid of the shadow of his many different faces.

In formal terms, therefore, I would say that a man can be properly attracted by a woman only when he has perceived and accepted his own femininity, and that a woman is ripe for being attracted by a man only when she has recognized and learned to tolerate her own masculinity. Of course, this syllogism should be taken with a pinch of salt. I have already explained that the notions of masculine and feminine are purely relative and very variable, and that in the development of normal human beings, there is no clear-cut distinction between the two. I would go so far as to say that the femininity that a man must recognize in himself before being open to the seductive influence of women is not something that can be described objectively or biologically, but something subjective, that is to say, a collection of traits and tendencies that, under the influence of his environment and his past, he is trying to get out of his system. In short, it is the negative image of himself that he is trying to transfer to members of the opposite sex. If he succeeds in fearlessly identifying this subjective femininity, consisting of all his undesired characteristics, he will cease to project it onto any women he meets. They in turn will be able to be feminine without frightening him. Only then will seductive influences be able to pass freely. Similarly, for a woman virility starts by being a synonym for all the undesired tendencies she carried within herself and which she gets rid of by transferring them to men. When she discovers enough self-confidence to examine her supposedly masculine tendencies without being afraid of their stimulating effects, she will cease to be afraid of men's mythical virility, which is only the reflection of her own. She will be able to differentiate men's real behavior—which is a mixture of generosity and egoism like her own

—from the mask that they wear rather obviously, and often with women's collusion, in order to emphasize those features which they think strengthen the idea of virility in them.

Once people begin to recognize themselves even down to their least-desired features, they will be less afraid of members of the opposite sex, who will stop being fearsome spooks and become individuals rather like themselves, no less attractive because they express the same personality conflicts—often in a complementary fashion. Fascination will give way to attraction: homosexuals are fascinated by women, whereas heterosexuals are attracted by them. This is the difference between myth and reality, between projections of oneself and the perception of real qualities in others.

VI

THE
LOVE RITUAL

Once they are ready to accept their partner's character as
it really is, couples can be more natural with each other.
But it is far from easy to define what is meant by "natural"
in this context. After the lengthy internal developments I
have described in previous chapters, it is as though individuals returned to the simplicity of mere biological reactions. When fear has been eliminated and harmony established between the partners' private worlds of the
unconscious, there should be nothing to prevent sexual approaches and sexual reactions from taking place naturally.
And yet, between the time when men and women become
attracted to one another and the time when they come together in a sexual relationship, they still go through a
whole range of behavior patterns and emotions. Only sim-
ple-minded or inhibited people try to avoid them, and if
they do so, they greatly weaken their final satisfaction. In

the normal course of human events, the sex act is preceded by a series of preliminaries, whose time scale will vary with the partners' knowledge of each other. I shall devote the next two chapters to describing the psychological meaning of these preliminaries. They cover attitudes that are not altogether obvious, and if either party refuses to accept them, there will be a collapse just before success is achieved. While the partners are still at the stage in which they base their judgment of the likelihood of successful sexual relations on the intensity of their mutual attraction, they naturally feel that nothing can cloud their pleasure. Their confidence will, however, decline when they have to start on the preliminaries. By themselves, these present no great difficulty: bringing a gift or offering a kiss does not require any special ability. If people find difficulty in these preliminary gestures of affection, it is because the gestures are the result of attitudes and sentiments that no one is able to experience at all times without some inner resistance.

Before defining these attitudes, I would like to explain more specifically what I mean by preliminaries. There are short-term and long-term preliminaries. The long-term ones are those that last through what is usually called the engagement period: exchanging courtesies, presents and visits. In passing, let me say that I am not necessarily attaching these acts to the institution of marriage and the preparations for it, since the same gestures can take place when two people are attracted to one another without wishing or without being able (perhaps because of a prior commitment) to come together in marriage. The man will take the woman out to dinner, and bring her flowers, perfume or candy. The woman will cook dinner for him, and give him presents suited to his activities or way of dressing. The short-term preliminaries are all those described in books on sexual behavior, and are mainly concerned with kisses and caresses. In this chapter I shall deal with the long-term preliminaries, leaving the short-term ones to the next chapter.

1

The whole series of behavior patterns that follow successful attraction, and whose purpose is to prepare the couple for mutual surrender, is summed up in one word: "courting." There is a long history behind this term. It comes from the Middle Ages of Western Europe and reflects a state of mind appropriate to an aristocratic society; for at that time "courtly love" was supposed to bind a knight or a troubadour to his beloved, not in a sexual or sensual manner, but in a way described by Nelli, an expert on Provençal love, as erotico-magical. According to Nelli, "A knight chose a lady, and identified himself with her, and gave her his friendship in order to enjoy in exchange the advantages of her beneficent magical aura."[1] Nelli's brilliant thesis starts from the notion that in early times, men considered women merely as objects of pleasure, and without some change in their sensitivities, could not feel for the women they desired the tenderness that as children they felt for their mothers. Thus, what was forbidden was not the sex act itself but the sex act combined with love: this would be tantamount to incest. Again, according to Nelli, men originally reserved their tendernesses for their mothers, while expecting sexual pleasure from the women they bought or captured, but never loved. This was the original form of male "consciousness." To be bold enough to love a woman other than his mother, or to concentrate on the woman of his choice not only his sexual desires but

[1] René Nelli, L'Amour et les mythes du coeur [Love and Love Myths], Paris, Hachette, 1952, p. 84.

also his feelings of tenderness, required, in Nelli's view, that the man first undergo a series of psychological changes. The main one was a sort of identification with the woman in question. Before loving a woman, a man had first to awaken his own latent femininity. It was by loving a woman "passionately," as though this were predestined, that the man ceased to have the feeling he was committing incest. In the real woman he was seeking a prop for his own ideal of femininity and motherhood. In this evolution, Nelli attaches prime importance to the magical ritual of the exchange of hearts: "This was a ritual of animistic communion in which the man's heart was considered to have entered into the bosom of his beloved, and that of the woman into the breast of her lover. The couple was thus bound indissolubly together, and formed a single human being. Everything that was felt by the one was simultaneously felt by the other."[2]

Nelli takes the historical approach and assumes that there is a parallel between the development of human sensitivity and that of literature, in which he is an acknowledged expert. This method of mixing psychology with literary history certainly raises a number of questions. It is, of course, tempting to see in the rolling stream of amorous poetic themes throughout the ages the main stages in the development of human sensitivity. But can such a parallel really be justified? Fortunately we are not concerned with this problem here, and I only want to talk about the magical significance of Nelli's "exchange of hearts." I believe that this rite was one way among many of expressing a psychological need that has existed since the beginning of time whenever the sort of tension that I have called sexual aggression has been generated between man and woman.

The man has to assimilate the woman's heart and the

2 *Ibid.*, p. 92.

woman the man's heart. The heart, like the blood, the spittle and the breath of the old texts, is a symbol of life. In consequence, the exchange of hearts represents a mutual offering of the whole self. Should we also consider it a ritual by
which the man acquires femininity and the woman virility?
This interpretation seems to me to involve rather elaborate
symbolism, and to have arisen through the development of
complex civilizations in which the essential, familiar acts
of love have become overlaid by academic metaphors far
removed from the primitive needs of the human soul.

What are these primitive needs? As was pointed out in
the last chapter, men have to start by ceasing to be afraid
of women, and women of men. Before they can experience
sexual attraction, the members of each sex have to stop seeing the other through the distorting mirror of their fantasies. The exchange of hearts is a symbol connected with
this world of fantasy. It represents an exchange of gifts side
by side with the death of the self. In it, love is connected
with death, wounds and blood. But the true gift starts only
after this frightening but fascinating symbolization has
taken place. The exchange of hearts is an expression in poetic form of a much more primitive exchange, both simpler
and closer to the psychological needs of men and women
who wish to allow themselves to be attracted by their partners, and so achieve carnal possession of them.

In the same way, "to go courting" is a historical and literary expression whose origins also lie in the realms of fantasy. The man pays allegiance to the lady of his heart, as a
vassal does to his overlord or a courtier to his king. These
images, spread by troubadours and poets heavily influenced
by their social environment, are like a verbalization, applicable to all lovers, of the simpler and more primitive
acts of nascent love. But it is essential to distinguish carefully between the images and the reality for which they
stand. The images depend very largely on the period in

which they are created: in an age of witchcraft and animism, they may take the form of a magical union of hearts; in the feudal period, of vassaldom; in royal times, allegiance; and madness at the time of the split between reason and unreason in the nineteenth century: the images reflect the fashion of the times. But although there can be no reality without the images, the reality is more lasting than they, and always leads back to a psychological need inherent in the unfolding of love and its successful conclusion.

In order to understand the underlying meaning of these images, we would do well to examine the forms of behavior that exist in primitive societies as well as in our own. There, lovers bring each other food, works of art, shells or jewels, or even the trophies of war. Margaret Mead writes about the Arapesh: "As a father's claim to his child is not that he has begotten it but rather that he has fed it, so also a man's claim to his wife's attention and devotion is not that he has paid a bride-price for her, or that she is legally his property, but that he has actually contributed the food which has become flesh and bone of her body. A little girl is betrothed when she is seven or eight to a boy about six years her senior, and she goes to live in the home of her future husband. Here the father-in-law, the husband, and all of his brothers combine to grow the little bride. Upon the young adolescent husband particularly falls the onus of growing yams, working sago, hunting for meat, with which to feed his wife. In later years, this is the greatest claim that he has upon her. If she is dilatory or sulky or unwilling, he can invoke this claim: 'I worked the sago, I grew the yams, I killed the kangaroo that made your body. Why do you not bring in the firewood?' "[3] Here is a marriage scheme very different from our own, most remarkable for the fact

[3] Margaret Mead, *Sex and Temperament in Three Primitive Societies*, New York, Dell Publishing Co., Inc., 1968, p. 90.

that the bond which forms the union and gives it strength is not the exchange of a girl for a given price, but the behavior of the young husband who for years provided the food "that has become part of her body." The phrase is very suggestive, with its allusion to a maternal role for the husband.

In another work Margaret Mead says that when the Samoans return from fishing, "the young fishermen separate out the 'Taboo fish,' which must be sent to the chief, or proudly they pack the little palm leaf baskets with offerings of fish to take to their sweethearts."[4] It is significant that the gift to the chief precedes the gift to the girls. Comparing these behavior patterns with those in the days of chivalry, when men "courted" women, we are bound to conclude that in the preliminaries of love, it is normal to adopt customs that reflect a "dominant-submissive" pattern. The young woman is given to understand by her lover that he stands in the same relationship to her as he does to the chief, the overlord or the king, depending on the social structure.

In these rites of symbolic allegiance, food plays a major part: the young men bring sago, yams, rice bread, wheat (as peasants do to their landowners), pastry or sweets. Regardless of the individual customs, which depend on the local produce, there is one permanent feature: whatever is offered as first fruits to the chief or as a gift to the fiancée or mistress must be the best of its sort, and the most agreeable to the palate. In poor societies, a fine rice cake may be a handsome gift, while in our society, where we have nearly everything, nobody would ever dream of offering a loaf of bread or a slice of meat.

Even when the gift consists not of food but of shells or

[4] Margaret Mead, *Coming of Age in Samoa*, New York, Dell Publishing Co., Inc., 1968, p. 28.

jewelry, it must still be a luxury item and it must be something out of the ordinary. If it is in any sense useful, it must be decorated with purely useless ornaments. The more common something is, the less it can be used as a gift, so that we run into the concepts of price and value.

And yet these cannot be followed too far. To offer money, the instrument of trade, would be considered very unsuitable at this stage of the proceedings. In a marriage contract, which is intended to fix the rights and duties of each of the parties, an exchange or pooling of physical goods does not upset anyone, at least in individualist societies like ours: by this time, after all, the partners are assumed to have reached emotional harmony. But regardless of the customs, habits or laws on matrimony, there seems to be one general rule: nobody can win a partner's affection and favors by gifts of money or of an object normally used in trade. If sexual intercourse takes place purely on a *quid pro quo* basis, that is prostitution; prostitution is precisely a form of trade in which physical pleasure is exchanged for an amount of money determined by the laws of supply and demand. It is perhaps worth inquiring why prostitution is both so unsatisfactory and so widespread. It would seem that neither partner attains the pleasure people have a right to expect from sexual intercourse. We have already discussed one of the reasons for this: in most cases the whole expressive side of love is missing. We are now in a position to add that the predominance of the trading aspect of the transaction and the absence of the ritual preliminaries, requiring the exchange of gifts, leave both the man and the woman unsatisfied.

It is here that we come to the significance of the preliminaries. When exchanging gifts, human beings are really not pursuing some transitory economic end. Rather, they are seeking an assurance of mutual devotion that will not be at the mercy of passing whims and needs. No doubt the young woman sees the gift as well worth having, but more important, it means that the man who seeks her hand is prepared to give her something to which he is greatly attached, and that he is prepared to move out of the world of economic calculation, where what is given is weighed against what is received, into physical and moral spheres where it is more blessed to give than to receive. Offering a gift is a symbolic act meaning that aggressiveness is finally vanquished by sympathy and love. Its purpose is to soften the beloved's anxieties about the morrow and what it will bring forth. By offering gifts that are not related to daily use, and which exceed anything that could be expected on the basis of fair exchange, the lover explains to his beloved that his aggressiveness toward her is a thing of the past, not only now, when he is sexually excited by her, but forever and a day, regardless of the vicissitudes of life. The exchange of gifts is thus not only an act of pacification but also a commitment for the future.

The Greek term for engagement, *engyesis,* expresses this very clearly. It comes from the verb *engyo,* meaning to offer a pledge or hand something over as a guarantee. The *engye* is the thing that is offered for this purpose. This etymology reminds me of a gesture that is still used in deals between merchants in certain agricultural areas of the world. When a deal has been worked out verbally, in order to prevent either of the parties from going back on their word before the exchange actually takes place, a solemn commitment is entered into. Each of the parties spits into his right hand, then they slap their right palms together. From then on the bargain is sealed. It is as if the spittle, something living from within each of them, has been exchanged by a ritual of wider significance than the transaction itself, thus giving it a stability it would not otherwise have. It seems likely that the Greeks considered marriage engagements to be consecrated by pledges of this sort, which gave the exchange between the girl's family and the boy's a permanent quality, implying that there could be no withdrawal. Naturally conventions of this sort are only applicable in societies where marriage is based on agreements between families. But it is reasonable to assume that with the advent of individualism, the partners took it upon themselves to make these ritual gestures which imply a pledge for the future and a promise of lasting peace.

Taking Mauss' splendid *Essai sur le don [Essay on Gifts]* as his starting point, Lévi-Strauss in one of his characteristically brilliant commentaries shows that both in primitive societies and in our own "a mysterious advantage attaches to obtaining commodities—or at any rate some commodities—by means of an exchange of gifts rather than by producing them or acquiring them individually,"[5] and he offers as examples "those great exchange operations" that occur each year in connection with Christmas, the New Year or Easter. "In our society," he says, "it is just as if certain non-essential consumer goods to which we attach great psychological, aesthetic or sensual significance, like flowers, candy and luxury goods, are considered as being correctly acquired by mutual exchange rather than by purchase for individual consumption."[6] In his explanation of these exchanges—whose economic result is nil, since the giver receives as much as he gives—Lévi-Strauss speaks of the attainment of moral goals, the establishment of a friendly atmosphere, and the reduction of tension. He describes a custom he has observed in southern France, and which he quotes as typical of many similar practices. Two strangers are eating at the same table in a small restaurant. Each of them orders his own food and pays for what he

5 Lévi-Strauss, *Les Structures élémentaires de la parenté,* Paris, P.U.F., 1949, p. 70.
6 *Ibid.,* p. 71.

eats, but this does not apply to the wine, a precious fluid used for showing friendship or for honoring someone. One of the diners pours wine from his bottle for the other, who promptly returns the gesture. Lévi-Strauss asks: "What is going on? The two bottles hold exactly the same amount, and the wine seems to be of the same quality. Neither of the two parties in this revealing scene has received anything more than if he had drunk from his own bottle. Economically speaking, no one has gained and no one has lost. But there is more value in exchanges than the value of the things exchanged."[7] What is this additional value? The two men are not enemies, but they *are* strangers. "There is a conflict, faint but nonetheless real and sufficient to create a state of tension in the two men, between the usual circumstance of solitude and the momentary fact that they are in company. They feel alone and yet together; they are constrained to adopt the reserve usual between strangers, while their physical situation vis-à-vis one another and the utensils laid out for the meal suggest, and even to some extent demand, close intimacy. . . . The exchange of wine enables them to escape from this ephemeral but difficult situation. It is an affirmation of goodwill that dissipates the feeling of uncertainty in both parties and replaces mere proximity by a positive bond."[8] Moving on from this minor but nevertheless suggestive observation to the customs of the Nambicuara Indians, whom he was able to observe in Western Brazil, the author describes small groups of nomads who fear and avoid each other, but who are obliged to make contact for reasons of trade. "There is a link, and even a logical connection, between hostile relationships and the mutual exchange of gifts. For the exchanges represent wars which have been settled by peaceful means, and

[7] *Ibid.*, p. 75.
[8] *Ibid.*, p. 76.

the wars represent transactions that have gone wrong. This interpretation is supported by the fact that the change from war to peace, or at least from hostility to cordiality, takes place by means of ritual acts representing a veritable inspection prior to reconciliation. The adversaries feel each other all over, and with gestures which derive straight from the recent combats, inspect collars, earrings, bracelets, and feather ornaments while making appreciative comments. This inspection, which is halfway between a state of war and a state of peace, is followed in the end by an exchange of gifts in complete silence, without any bargaining, with no expression of satisfaction or complaint, and with no apparent relationship between what is offered and what is received."[9]

Lévi-Strauss' purpose in expanding on Mauss' *Essay on Gifts* was to show that in primitive societies the mutual exchange of gifts plays an important part in the organization of marriage. Women, precious above all other possessions, are exchanged for other women; this exchange prevents tribes from shutting themselves in on themselves, and is thus at the very basis of social existence. Lévi-Strauss summarizes this tempting theory in the following way: "There is an unbroken transition from war to trade, and from trade to marriage; and the exchange of women in betrothal is only the end of an uninterrupted process of mutual giving and receiving which makes it possible to shift from hostility to partnership, from anxiety to confidence, and from fear to friendship."[10] My reason for mentioning Lévi-Strauss' theory here is not sociological but psychological. I would like to inquire whether these gestures of mutual appeasement do not have the same meaning when they occur between a man and a woman, drawn together but still mu-

[9] *Ibid.,* p. 86.
[10] *Ibid.*

tually fearful, as they have when they are practiced by two mistrustful tribes.

In society, not only families mistrust each other and have to be appeased by an exchange of gifts, but individuals, too, are afraid of one another, especially when they are of the opposite sexes. I have analyzed this fear in the preceding chapter, and I have shown that it is based on latent aggression which leaves its mark on both parties, even after the long process of working out the original sexual aggression is completed. Once a man has been attracted to a woman, the two still have to find a way of warding off any chance of a rebirth of hostility. This seems to me the meaning of the whole love ritual; it is designed to exorcise fear, anxiety and all the other foes of a successful union. Before the partners can abandon themselves to each other entirely, they must have an assurance that at least in principle there will be no more aggression between them, and that such aggressive feelings as remain will be used only to fight off external dangers, and to ensure their joint preservation. Gifts are the device human beings invent as a method of saying that they wish to leave selfish considerations aside, and that they are prepared to try to look after someone else's interests and pleasures as if they were their own.

Perhaps I shall be told that this special significance of gifts and courting is not of the slightest interest to those actually concerned. When they exchange rings and gifts the engaged pair would hardly think of the meaning that we believe attaches to their actions. They do these things because it is the custom to do them: "That's what you do when you are in love." This is an interesting line of criticism, especially because it is partly true and partly false. It is true that the people who do these things are often ignorant of their meaning, and are certainly unlikely to have the kind of detailed knowledge of their significance that a scientific observer might possess. It is also true that most of the conduct connected with courting is related, even when the participants do not know it, to customs which have their origins in antiquity and in religion. I would go even further and say that when men and women begin courting, love at last becomes part of social conduct, in the psychological sense of the term. Individuals emerge from their personal emotions or feelings, and from their very subjective mutual attraction, and they abstract from the old customs their most poignant and valuable features. It seems likely, indeed, that most of the rites connected with courting were originally forms of behavior in use between groups of young men making peace or swearing eternal loyalty, and that these customs were afterward taken over by individuals wishing to obtain the favors of a partner. In this connection I would like to recall the behavior of the young Samoan fishermen when they return in the evening from a successful day's fishing: they start by setting aside the taboo fish for the chief; then they take certain other fish and use them for filling little baskets which they offer at nightfall to the girls they are courting. The relationship between social customs, with their political overtones, and the behavior of individuals intent on seduction is perfectly clear: in order to win the attention of his girl the young man pays her the homage that is usually reserved for the head of the tribe. The same behavior that is in one instance a sign of political obligation, can be in another a matter of free choice and desire.

But if individuals and couples choose their social conduct, whether political or not, they do so for very clear-cut reasons, even if they do not clearly understand what the reasons are. Their purpose is to disarm the other person, and to eliminate the defensive attitudes that remain despite the mutual attraction. For this purpose they use gestures, behavior and words that remind the partner of stable relationships, like those of a mother and her child, a suze-

rain and his vassal, a king and a courtier, or even a mad-
man and the focus of his own particular form of madness.
All these relationships, whose common feature is their
durability and closeness, can be useful to individuals as
symbols intended to prove that one's partner need no
longer be afraid of a lack of stability, and can count on a
lasting union.

I spoke earlier of anxiety. Modern philosophers have
shown that basically all human beings are full of anxieties.
They are worse off than animals; not only do they suffer
the blows of fate—cold and heat, hunger, sickness, old age
and death—but they remember the ills they have suffered
and are able to anticipate all the misfortunes that are likely
to befall them. They even anticipate their own death,
which is perhaps the main source of their anxiety. With
their memories and forebodings, they are always in a state
of anxiety, and it is certainly for this reason that they take
greater precautions than any animal to ward off misfor-
tune. Because he is extremely egotistical, man is suspicious
of his neighbor, whom he knows to be human like himself.
Before handing over his body to someone else in a state of
nakedness that symbolizes the surrender of any weapons
he may possess, he must go through a long and calming series of rituals, whose sole purpose is to provide an assurance
of lasting devotion.

As human beings do not live only in the mind, the beloved will not be satisfied with just a set of words. For
words are easy enough to say, and they may hide intentions
just as easily as they reveal them. The words which the beloved wishes to hear are both solemn and ritual. They must
not contain the casual note used in daily chatter, bargaining or political persuasion. They must have a sort of liturgical style, whose purpose is to emphasize the permanent
nature of the hoped-for relationship and of the accompanying devotion. It is not by chance that the great religious

texts of mankind speak the language of love. For this language has a ritual character of its own that makes it suitable for expressing the realities that transcend the vagaries
of daily life. The words used in "courting" are formalized
in a way that places them outside the realm of individual
whim. If they are properly to express the ritual meaning
that, hopefully, they bear, they must have the same shine
and glitter and peculiarly precious nature that ought to be
found in actual gifts, whether of food or other objects. This
glitter, like that of gold or pearls, is a symbol of permanence and durability in contrast to the consumable nature
of current commodities.

2

The main themes used by the language of love to assuage
the anxieties of the beloved and offer an assurance of stability are borrowed, as I have said, from the realities of society or of nature. I shall take a few of the most significant
of these themes and discuss them in turn. I would like to
repeat that they change from era to era. As soon as one lot
is worn out or loses its meaning, others are invented; the
new ones usually scandalize the elders and give the younger
set great pleasure.

   a. For my first theme I shall go back to the example of
the Arapesh. In that tribe, where marriages are arranged by
their families while the boys and girls are still very young,
the real basis of the marriage is felt by the couple to be the
fact that the husband provided food for his wife, which became the flesh and bones of her body. These primitive and
moving themes suggest the idea that a man is like a mother
to his wife, and that the bond between them is as close as
that linking a mother to the child of her flesh. It is the
same symbolism which makes the description of the birth

of Eve, the first woman and the first wife, from the rib of Adam, the first man, so profoundly important.

Some psychoanalysts have concluded that this symbolism means that any man taking a woman wishes to identify himself with his mother. And if a man turns out to be incapable of choosing a partner and courting her, they will explain that because of his youthful conflicts with his mother he can no longer identify with her, and so is incapable of adopting a sufficiently maternal attitude to make courting possible. Although this explanation may not be entirely wrong, it does not seem to me to be complete. It is concerned with the expression of desires, and completely leaves out the question of intention. The mother-child relationship is a symbol intended to signify a deeper devotion of man to woman than that normally involved in daily business relations between two adults. If some people are unable to offer symbols of this sort to potential partners, it is because they are still too full of hostility toward them. They would feel altogether too hypocritical if they introduced such meaningful symbolism into their words or deeds.

b. At the other end of the scale of civilizations, and contrasting with the primitive image of a woman formed out of the rib of a man, we come across another very plausible-sounding theme, that of returning to one's mother. Those who read Sándor Ferenczi's ingenious essay entitled *Psychoanalysis of the Origins of Sex Life*[11] will see how research that was originally intended to be scientific and objective can gradually turn into something just as symbolic and grandiose as the great myths of the human race. The author, who was a friend and faithful disciple of Freud, shows that the "act of copulation is really an expression of

[11] Dr. Sándor Ferenczi, *Thalassa, psychanalyse des origines de la vie sexuelle,* translated from the Hungarian by N. Abraham, Paris, Payot, 1962. (Originally published in 1923.)

the desire to return to the mother's womb."[12] His essay contains his complete theory regarding the universality of the desire for return to the mother and its fulfillment in the act of coitus,[13] "an act which makes possible a real if partial return to the mother's uterus."[14] Extending his thesis to cover the whole animal kingdom throughout the inhabited world, he even manages to write: "In the end the higher vertebrates have succeeded in organizing internal fertilization and development inside the mother's body, thus successfully uniting this form of parasitic existence with the desire to return to the sea."[15] In order to explain this last remark, the author says that "the mother is really the symbol of the ocean, or its partial substitute, and not the other way round."[16] Consequently, according to him, all adult individuals really wish to escape from their state of separateness, and to return, either in fact or in fancy, to the source of their origins, none other than the great Ocean, mother of all living beings.

I would be very surprised if many biologists showed much interest in these "bioanalytical" observations. And psychoanalysts, used as they are to the fantastic constructions their patients produce, can only express their admiration. But there is a real danger that these symbols may be mistaken for a description of things as they really are. Ferenczi's descriptions are, of course, very like the visions of certain neurotics and psychotics. But they also contain one of the finest symbols men have attached to the sex act in their attempts to escape the limitations of the fleeting instant. To represent the act of copulation as a partly real, partly imaginary, return to the mother's womb is surely one of the

12 *Ibid.,* p. 46.
13 *Ibid.,* p. 56.
14 *Ibid.,* p. 48.
15 *Ibid.,* p. 93.
16 *Ibid.*

most solemn possible ways of conferring sanctity on a
purely biological act, and so of releasing it from the limitations of the present moment and the imperfections of
capricious desire. I am sure that no psychoanalyst will take
me to task if I suggest that many psychoanalytical theories,
instead of being content with describing the fantasies of
the unconscious, also provide mankind with new and ap-
pealing symbols, often almost liturgical in content, which
members of future generations will doubtless use to explain to their partners their firm intention of giving their
relationship some greater significance than they give to
the profit-ridden actions of daily life.

   c. Between these two great symbols of the sex relationship—woman born from the rib of Adam, and man returning to his mother's womb—are many others which have
been popular at one time or another. In the Western world,
which was born under feudalism and weaned under mon-
archy, those connected with allegiance have predominated:
courting, being the slave of the man or the woman, dying
for the beloved, etc. However, as all these symbols are well
known, I shall only comment on a current one, which I
have found in perhaps its most developed form in Chris-
tiane Rochefort's novel *Le Repos du guerrier* [*The War-
rior's Rest*], where it occurs with a clarity that is cruel and
even scandalous. The reader cannot help being shocked by
this masochistic story of a girl from a good middle-class
family who becomes the servile mistress of a young sot
whose main activities are drinking and making love to her.
This is hardly the model to set before the young, any more
than were the madness and *liebestot* of the literature of
the romantic period. Nevertheless, we must admit that a
novel like this certainly provides a powerful and meaningful symbol of the love relationship, even if it is borrowed
from the worlds of madness and perversion. For masochists
and perverts are bound to the objects of their affection in

a manner so disturbing as to become fascinating in itself and thus capable of representing the desire for permanence in the love relationship. Men and women who wish to give the relationship they offer their partners more stability than the relationships of everyday life, and to offer their partners some assurance of devotion through thick and thin, will not hesitate to use even the most pathological bonds as symbols or metaphors.

Thus, the courting phase is one of a continuous exchange of gifts and words whose chief feature may be said to be hyperbole. Everything is directed toward fulfilling a ritual, the purpose of which is to calm the partners' fears by assuring them that their wooers are offering all that is best in themselves and that their interest is more than merely transitory; the hope is to establish a link as permanent as that between a child and its mother, a knight and his suzerain, a drunkard and his bottle. At this stage of development, the images expressing the desires of the unconscious turn into symbols, or rather, into symbolic actions offering pledges for the future.

For the benefit of those who are not convinced by this analysis of the meaning of the preliminaries to love, I would like to conclude this chapter with one clinical observation. Some young men in love are miserable because they cannot bring themselves to offer a gift or make a declaration. This terrible psychological paralysis is at the root of a great deal of wretchedness and of many acts of despair, which well-balanced people find hard even to imagine. Superficial analysts are likely to conclude that the young men in question are afraid of the outcome of their relationship, which would normally be sexual intercourse. Because, as a result of their perverse or incestuous tendencies, the young men consider intercourse sinful, they feel they must prevent it, and so they avoid courting, which would be bound to lead them in what they feel to be the wrong direction. But such an analysis is altogether too black and white. It attributes to purely hypothetical forebodings an inhibition whose real explanation is to be found in the conflicts aroused by the situation itself. Serious analysis will show that these young men's attitude to women is thoroughly ambivalent: they find them attractive, but become distinctly hostile as soon as they show any resistance. Torn in this way between desire and hate, they dare not give vent to their feelings. Furthermore—and this is the crux of the matter—they are likely to consider the ritual acts connected with courting as mere hypocrisy which would quickly be seen through by the person being courted. They are not sufficiently relieved of aggression in their own minds to be able to produce the behavior and words which would convince their potential partners that they intend to offer lasting affection. Still worse, they are too fond of their own hostility to want to go through the rites of peace with any woman. They are in fact in the position of many sinners who are still so attached to their sins that they deliberately avoid any purifying or peace-bringing liturgical process on the grounds that to take part in it would only be hypocritical.

Human beings whose initial aggressions have melted away and who are prepared to recognize aggressive feelings when they reappear from time to time, without either being frightened or losing their self-esteem, will have no difficulty in making up their minds to use the hyperbole of love. They will make use of ritual gifts and hallowed words to overcome any fear or hostility their partners, or they themselves, may feel. Even if the partners feel that the future may still produce conflicts and divergences of feeling between them, they will have enough self-confidence and enough belief in the strength of the rituals of pacification not to withdraw from a self-surrender that has to be virtually permanent.

VII

THE CONSUMMATION OF
THE SEX ACT

Two human beings who start by being hostile to each other, and then progress through mistrust and timidity to trust and confidence, finally reach the immediate preliminaries of the sex act, traditionally called love play, or the prelude to love.

People who have not had an experience of sex are often anxious as to whether they will know what to do, or whether they will conduct themselves properly. This attitude seems to me astonishing on two counts. First, what is complicated about a kiss or an embrace? And second, why should anyone fear that they will be met with disdain or mistrust by someone whom they approach with the timidity of a novice? We shall see the deeper reason for this apprehension a bit later. I would like first to comment on the behavior of lovers who, uncertain of their powers, sometimes thumb hastily through books on the technique of love-making.

Plenty of such works have been produced in any period you care to name. Some of them are vulgar, others more discreet; they cover the whole range from pornography, where everything is indicated by suggestion in order to give the impotent reader "instant stimulation," to science, or what passes for science. But all of them without exception are spoiled by the explicit or implicit assumption that physical love is only a matter of technical skill. This attitude betrays a complete misunderstanding of the meaning of the preliminary acts.

It is useful, of course, for a young man to know that a woman takes longer than he does to reach the state of excitement that produces orgasm; that both his body and hers contain some areas that are more easily excitable than others; and that the relative positions of their bodies can be varied to provide additional pleasure. But it should also be understood that only rarely are people who suffer from impotence, premature ejaculation or frigidity in the dark about the various love-making techniques. On the contrary, they usually know more about them than anyone else, and this is surely proof that failure is less a matter of proficiency than of desire. It sometimes happens that a couple who have been relatively happy or satisfied for years suddenly find that they cannot have agreeable relations: the woman has no pleasure and the man arrives too quickly. Are we to say that this couple has forgotten the techniques, or that the partners have lost their skill? This seems most unlikely. Inquiry will probably reveal that what has actually happened is that the feelings of one or the other of them have changed, perhaps as a result of an affair on the side, and that this has shut off or distorted reactions that in the past were simple and straightforward. This happens to many couples approaching middle age. They have not so much forgotten how to embrace as how to love. If an older person finds a younger partner, his or her abilities return on the spot. One of the reasons many people prefer to consider love-making a matter of technique is that this enables them to avoid involving their emotions, which are much more difficult to handle.

1

We should try to agree on what we mean by the verb "to love." There are many couples living harmoniously together, each partner generous to the other, who would pull a sour face if anyone suggested that love was by itself sufficient to ensure good sexual relations; and they would go on to describe their own vainly repeated efforts to reach mutual satisfaction. One answer to this objection—a serious one that ought to be borne in mind by all who write on sex and love from the point of view of religious morality—is that love is neither a recipe nor a technique. The whole purpose of my analysis is to show that successful sexual union is something that cannot be brought about merely by conscious love or burning passion. In human beings, at least, it requires a long internal process: the elimination of perverse elements, the purifying expression of conflicts in the unconscious, the declaration of emotions and feelings, and the completion of the preliminary rites. When I say that a prerequisite for the uninhibited movements that compose the prelude to the love act is a state of grace traditionally called love, I mean that it requires a special psychophysiological state of the whole organism, and a general pliability of the psyche: it is this that permits expression without affectation, false shame, and undue excess, and thus gradually leads to surrender—not to licence, which is only a caricature of sexual freedom. Anyone wishing to understand what is needed for physical harmony must first distinguish between love as an emotion and love as an ideal, a state that is never actually reached, but which is gradually approached by two partners who periodically succeed in discharging the tension that keeps them apart—and never ceases to do so, whatever they may think —without recourse to violence. Love as an emotion is no more than one of the intermediate stages, though an indispensable one, along the path followed by two people as they come together. But it can exist even though love as an ideal is never reached. It can also exist along with many deep unconscious hesitations, and it may even go hand in hand with narcissism. If anyone fails to surmount any one of these obstacles, he or she will run into difficulties further along the road.

Personally, I have often been surprised by the insistence with which many eminent specialists in sexual matters have asserted that in this field human beings cannot lie to themselves. For example, Oswald Schwarz, one of the most eminent and most subtle psychologists of sex, repeats like a refrain that "sex is the only function that cannot lie."[1] He means that unlike other spheres of life, where we can always make good our weaknesses, conceal our inadequacies, or get by more or less successfully by playing a part, sexual relations reveal people to each other as they really are. The argument is that with such a close degree of intimacy, no mask will stay in place. Astonished by such an unequivocal statement, which nevertheless appears to be confirmed by daily clinical experience, I set out to try to discover why it should be true. The preceding pages are the results of my research. If two people who enjoy each other's embraces cannot achieve complete and guiltless sexual satisfaction unless they are sincerely and deeply in love, this can only be because the human body, like an instrument of extreme perfection, is sensitive to the slightest latent tendencies, the

[1] Oswald Schwarz, *Psychology of Sex*, Penguin, London, 1967.

most insignificant twinges of the unconscious, the most fleeting emotions and even the most hidden unavowed reluctance in the mind.

Must we therefore conclude that only someone who has cleansed himself of every aggressive element so that his love is perfect, indeed almost angelic, can expect to experience complete sexual enjoyment? Surely not, for that would be to accept a new heresy akin to that of the Cathars, who rejected all physical love because they believed that even in the most favorable circumstances it always retained some fragments of evil, or a taint of sin, that could only be avoided by those who achieved pure and spiritual love. We might say that all those sexual psychologists who demand (as a prerequisite for a successful sex act) the final disappearance of hostility between the sexes, or the blossoming of a completely homogeneous spiritual love, are our contemporary Cathars. If taken too literally, some of Schwarz's phrases seem to me to be tending toward this modern form of Manichaeism.

What is really needed as psychological preparation for the most successful blossoming of the human sex act is the replacement of real aggression by harmless aggression. Inside ourselves, we must each play out to a successful conclusion the game of love against hate. We have already seen how man's capacities of expression and imagination can strip sexuality of its perverse, egoistical and dangerous features. The point is that the free and innocent expression of the conflicts inherent in all sexuality must be carried over into the most intimate aspects of any union. If a relationship falls apart, it is because one of the perverse features of the original sexuality has remained too strong to find expression in sex play. What people take to bed with their partner, and rightly so, is neither a soul washed clean of all trace of egoism, nor a mind entirely devoted to the other, but their whole being, complete with fears and anxieties, demands and pleasures, greed and devotion—in other words, the complete man or woman—imbued with a heightened but serene tension which permits the free use of all that is in the psyche. It is not by chance that the ancient world represented love in the form of a childlike cupid armed with darts, thus creating a symbol of a war that is both harmless and exciting, nor that most languages refer to the preliminaries to love as a game in which all the impulses of the individuals concerned are freely expressed without any real danger, in order to bring about the necessary mutual stimulation. If we say that love must be present in any sex relationship that is to be entirely satisfactory, this means that there must be no *serious* aggression, not that there must be none of those subtle games in which aggression turns into its converse, which is amorous stimulation. As soon as either body shows any real hostility, nothing more can be done to achieve the hoped-for mutual surrender. The only possible outcome in those circumstances is a sado-masochistic relationship. It is to avoid such an outcome that some people back out of any love play and return to their internal development processes both to reduce the intensity of their aggressive feelings, and to give them that playful quality which converts them from obstacles to love into factors contributing to pleasurable sexual excitement.

There is no point in giving detailed descriptions to back up this interpretation of the preliminaries to the love act. I am sure that all my readers will have understood my allusions to the details of love play, which include tooth nips, kisses, controlled but violent hugs, joking abuse, pretenses of being afraid or hurt and so forth. I do not feel that this is a taboo subject, but it *is* difficult to discuss, because it relates to everything that is most intimate and necessarily most childish in the adventure of sex. To speak of it at length or in detail would be a devious form of exhibitionism or voyeurism. The nearer we get to the climax of sexual tension, the less ordinary language can do to give a clear description of what takes place. It should withdraw, as it does with all couples who reach the point where they cast aside their internal visions, anticipations and imaginings, and even their declarations of affection, to let their bodies speak for them.

In normal circumstances there are no spectators at these events, nor should there be. Only voyeurs try to look through the keyhole. But sometimes children who have been kept too long in their parents' bedroom, because in cramped family quarters there is nowhere else for them to go, are witnesses to these embraces which seem so odd to them at their tender age. And even if children do not actually see their parents at their love play, they try to imagine what goes on, although to do so may make them unhappy. They do this because they are fascinated by what Freud called the "primal scene." He believed that young children interpret what they see in terms of a violent struggle, as if their parents were fighting to the death. I mention this Freudian theory only because it illustrates one aspect of the prelude to the sex act—i.e., that the preliminaries contain elements of controlled and mastered violence—and it is thus not at all surprising that inexperienced witnesses of the events should see them as a battle between the strong, the father, and the weak, the mother. The child's interpretation of sex relations, which is echoed by the reaction of many adults when they see dogs or cats copulating, has a very real basis in fact, for the partners are engaged in an amorous struggle. What is wrong with the interpretation is that the witnesses take the struggle at its face value, when it is in fact only a sort of drama intended to raise the level of the emotions.

We have now reached a position that is exactly the converse of that with which we started this book. For the reader will remember that we started with someone experiencing strong erotic stimulation but unable to react because of external prohibitions. Their sexual feelings were infected by real and possessive aggressiveness, to which they were completely subordinate. The most visible proof of this took the form of perversions, in which tendencies to fight, attack and destroy became predominant themes in the tension caused by the erotic stimuli. But when psychosexual development is complete, the position is the other way around, for if the aggressive elements have not entirely disappeared, they have been brought under control, and are only of secondary importance. Once they have been mastered, they are used by the partners just sufficiently to obtain the ideal tension in their bodies, without ever turning pleasure into pain.

The turnabout is so complete that if we are to use language correctly, we can hardly speak of aggression any more. For neither of the partners wishes to use mouth, hands, arms, legs or thighs to bring about the other's destruction. At the start of love play, they may pretend to do so, but this is only to increase the tension in the partner's body. Gradually, moreover, the idea of attack or possession disappears and gives way to gentle rhythmic movements whose sole purpose is to raise the tension of the whole system, first in the outer organs and then closer and closer to the sexual apparatus itself. It is at this point rather than at the beginning of an analysis of sexuality that it would seem reasonable to describe the muscular system of the reproductive organs, and its role in copulation. Such a description would show that the result of caresses that start with the most ordinary parts of the body farthest removed from the sex organs is a general tension that works gradually toward the genitals themselves.

2

In the preliminaries, the caress plays a predominant part. Of all forms of human behavior, it is one of the most specific. In the first place, it is performed by the hand, which has become extremely flexible in human beings, and is now a far more delicate instrument than is to be found in any other animal, except, perhaps, in rudimentary form in monkeys. A human being's hand can reach any part of someone else's body and fit every shape and form. In the hand are concentrated all the powers of gesture of the whole body. In the second place, it is clear that the caress is the most intimate and most conspicuous demonstration of respect for someone else, for the hand that is mostly used to constrain and compel has now become an instrument of love, of infinite inventiveness, at the service of the erotic demands of a body other than our own. In itself, without the need for wit or imagination, the caress is a sure evidence of identification with another. A part of one's body is used to give intense pleasure to another's—pleasure of a sort which individuals concerned only with their own satisfaction would not wish to bestow on anyone's body except their own. So to shake someone by the hand is not only a way of putting oneself symbolically in their power, it also means that one is prepared to put the most mobile and naturally dominating part of one's body at the other person's service.

The finest early example of a caress is to be found in the behavior of mothers. For mothers calm their children by gently caressing their hair, holding them by the hand and rocking them in their arms. This is a deep-seated, instinctive identification with both the suffering and the well-being of the living creature formed from the mother's womb.

Mothers feel their children's illnesses as if they were in their own bodies. This form of biological identification is most intense at the moment of birth, and becomes progressively weaker as the child grows up. Indeed, there is a risk of the child becoming a partner in sex if the mother's identification with the child is continued too long. The caresses of lovers naturally go further than those of mothers, and they are far more than the result of mere identification. If they were no more than that, or if people in caressing or letting themselves be caressed, were only living out a child-mother relationship like that of their early youth, their gestures of love would surely be clumsy and inhibited, as though they were infected by the fear of committing some sort of incestuous act. If it is true, as many authors assert, that men took many hundreds of years to decide to be kind and loving with their wives and mistresses, it is because they wrongly considered their mother's caresses, whose purpose was to calm and tranquilize, to be similar to the caresses that they exchanged with their women. While they had easily understandable subjective reasons for feeling like this, there was bound to be continued resistance between the partners as long as they did so. But as soon as the position was understood in its proper light, and women were accepted as partners and spouses, with equal rights in the use of their body, caresses could cease to be mothers' embraces intended to calm someone's pain or worries and become lovers' caresses whose whole purpose is to produce an agreeable tension in the body of a long-term partner.

In these circumstances, each partner is not merely identifying with the suffering or well-being of someone else, but with one of the most agreeable and life-giving tensions. One body excites the other in a harmony that involves far more than mere contact and is rooted in a biological connection that can very reasonably be called an identification

of one person with the other, so far as their bodies are concerned.

It will also be clear that people whose bodies remain
tense, with the gates closed against the rising tides of desire, will have difficulty in reaching enjoyment in the end.
In those circumstances, even if there is ejaculation or orgasm, it is against the wishes of the person concerned, and
without the willing participation of the whole system. Wil-
helm Reich, whose books contain a mixture of brilliant
ideas and nonsense, is said to have tried to give his frigid,
impotent or neurotic patients some way of expressing themselves with their bodies. He started by training them first
to use the facial muscles to laugh, show anger or cry; then
he went on to the muscles of the abdomen and finally to
those of the pelvis, which are the ones primarily involved
in sexual intercourse. If I understand Reich's technique
correctly, it was founded in his purpose, which was to enable people to relax bodies that had been frozen in defensive postures for many years. But I question his methods;
his patients' stiffness was surely more psychological than
physical in origin, and it seems to me that restoring a body
to its original state of suppleness is not so much a matter of
technique as of emotional reeducation. Make no mistake
about it: the rediscovery of the freedom of the muscles and
the senses is a long operation. Similarly, the simple and
natural use of one's own body in harmony with another,
equally relaxed and free, is not just a matter of will. It pre-
supposes the dissolution, at least for most of the time, of
the knots of aggression that are constantly reforming in
the psyche under the impact of the stresses of life, from
which no one is free.

3

Why do human beings, at least those who have not re-nounced sex life for honorable reasons, set such store on its success? Is it simply because of a passing itch in the genital organs? If this were so, there would be no real reason for the sadness that overcomes most people after they have masturbated or had intercourse with a prostitute. Are we overestimating men and women in thinking that they have at least a vague and rudimentary understanding of the deeper significance of truly successful intercourse? I believe that there is something fine and noble in most people's discontent with their sexual lives. Their restless pursuit of something different, and even their immoral behavior, are often the result of a desire for peace. What they are seeking down so many wrong paths is not simply physical pleasure for themselves, as is thought by many hard-line moralists, but peace with someone else—a peace that implies a temporary dissolution of their cores of hostility and is expressed in the freedom of two bodies entirely given over to each other at the moments of release. If they do not succeed in finding this peace of the body fairly regularly with someone who is entirely willing, there is likely to be a residue of anxiety, which leaves them extremely vulnerable to even the faintest suggestion of finding it elsewhere.

I do not want anyone reading these lines to accuse me of being an idealist. I would be falling into that error if I were to believe that humanity is likely ever to reach a condition where this peace and freedom of the body are permanent, having been acquired once and for all. I would be neurotically idealistic if I were to consider the most intimate desire of men and women—i.e., the desire for a lasting reconciliation of body and soul—as something that actually exists or as something that is easy to attain. I am sorry, but even if it costs me dear I would not willingly accept the views set out by Norman O. Brown in the lyrical pages of a book that was a best-seller in the United States sometime ago.[2] There he described, apparently in the full conviction of its possibility, a future period of human history when individuals would recover once and for all the free and joyful use of their bodies, and when they would finally accept the perverse polymorphism of their childhood in a sort of resurrection of the body: "We have already done what we could to extract from psychoanalytical theory a model of what the resurrected body would be like. The life instinct, or sexual instinct, demands activity of a kind that, in contrast to our current mode of activity, can only be called play. The life instinct also demands a union with others and with the world around us based not on anxiety and aggression but on narcissism and erotic exuberance. . . . At the same time—and here again Christian theology and psychoanalysis agree—the resurrected body is the transfigured body. The abolition of repression would abolish the unnatural concentrations of libido in certain particular bodily organs—concentrations engineered by the negativity of the morbid death instinct, and constituting the bodily base of the neurotic character disorders in the human ego. . . . The human body would become polymorphously perverse, delighting in that full life of all the body which it now fears."[3] These are very ambiguous lines; they are neither entirely true, nor entirely false, and they hint of gnosticism. For they imply that there would be a general conversion of humanity from its present state of extreme asceticism, or in modern jargon, from a civilization dominated by its repressions, to a completely amoral

[2] Norman O. Brown, *Life Against Death*, Middletown, Conn., Wesleyan University Press, 1959.
[3] *Ibid.*, pp. 307–308.

society, a Dionysiac society in which "the human physical senses must be emancipated from the sense of possession and then the humanity of the senses and the human enjoyment of the senses will be achieved for the first time."[4] These broad glimpses into the future are really no more than inspirational prophecies. Although they are based on a precise and penetrating understanding of the triumph over aggression represented by any successful act of sexual intercourse, they make such sex acts a model for all human activities. They envision knowledge, political life and indeed the whole of society as imbued with the purifying spirit of Eros, and moreover of an Eros accepted without fear and purified of any instinct for domination. I do not pretend to cover such a broad canvas in this little book. A successful sexual relationship in which the two partners are able to overcome their perverse tendencies, their narcissism and their fears, so that even if only briefly, they find freedom through a part of the body that is by its very nature directed toward a complementary part of another body, may indeed be seen as a symbol foreshadowing a society which has overcome the death instinct and all its progeny, such as mistrust, jealousy, envy, ambition and pride. But in fact mankind's political and economic relationships have their own laws and their own imperatives, which cannot be considered on the same footing as the problems of sex life. Indeed, the only real link between these various aspects of existence, some of which relate to the brain and the struggle for existence, others to the organs of reproduction and eroticism, is that each can be used as an analogy in describing the other. Only false prophets pretend that they are identical or even similar.

Psychoanalysts or psychologists dealing with sex like to keep within their own field; but here, too, Brown's rosy

4 *Ibid.,* p. 318.

and attractive conclusions are apt to lead us astray. For they
are based on the assumption that the sexual instinct can
permanently overcome the death instinct and cast it aside
like the husk of some outdated tyrant from the Bronze or
Iron Ages. How difficult it is for even the most enlightened
minds to forego the nostalgia of a Golden Age!

Without presuming to prophesy, I shall try to establish
what I think successful intercourse means for men and
women. It is not merely something like satisfying a bodily
hunger; indeed, it is most annoying to find this comparison with the appetite, which at first sight would seem to be
both helpful and natural in even the best books on sex
life. Human beings who copulate in the same spirit in
which they eat are surely not models of happiness. And to
write that sexual intercourse is like slaking one's thirst is
being neither realistic nor truly free. Most of the time all
it proves is that the author has quite misunderstood all the
varied factors that are inevitably involved in a sexual relationship between two individuals; or it is evidence of a
flight from the kind of emotional inadequacy which makes
it impossible for the author to attain the state of mind necessary for a healthy sex life. Now that we have disposed of
the comparisons with hunger and thirst, we still have to
deal with the biological meaning of sex, to which so much
importance was attached by the early psychoanalysts. Their
view was that sexual intercourse can be described simply
as a state of tension followed by an agreeable release. This
involves seeing things through the wrong end of the tele-
scope, that is to say, from the physiological end, and ignores
the fact that the state of tension is in itself rather agreeable
and satisfying—a point that, as a matter of fact, rather intrigued Freud himself. While it is true that the real meaning
of intercourse is to some extent concerned with the muscles
and with release of energy, it goes far deeper than that,
since the special feature of the sexual instinct is that it in-

volves two people. And these two people, who start by mis-
trusting one another before they come together, calm each
other's fears and finally pluck up courage to surrender
their bodies to each other in mutual identification.

Orgasm, which is the conclusion of an individual's sexual development, is the release that follows the height of
tension in the genital organs. Looked at psychologically
and subjectively, there is a sort of pleasure that spreads
throughout the whole body. And yet the moralists, copying
the naturalists, have a saying: *post coitum, animal triste*
(after coitus the animal is sad). If this is true of people who
have just had intercourse, it can only mean that all their
internal reservations had not yet been removed, that their
bodies had not yet achieved completely free self-expression,
and that parts both of the organism and of the psyche had
refused to perform their erotic roles. It may be said that
this explanation is bound to be discouraging for the many
people who are still afflicted by this well-known sadness.
This may be, but it is also a way of inviting them not to be
satisfied with their situations, and to open their eyes to the
real reasons for their lack of success, which are persistence
in an attitude of psychological rigidity, an undue attachment to their resentments and fears, and to their hatred
for their own bodies. It is also a way of encouraging them
to look for an ever-increasing love, despite the inevitable
difficulties of daily life, and to include bodily love in this
search, even though they may have been brought up to
consider it as degrading.

The German language has an excellent word to describe
the sex act, which may also be used to describe any instinctive action. This word is *Befriedigung,* meaning "pacification" or "appeasement." Both terms are evidence of the
existence of sharp apprehension about the significance of
the sex act. Nowadays we have lost this apprehension and,
in our pseudoscientific manner, call sex an instinctive mat-

THE CONSUMMATION OF THE SEX ACT

ter. But in so doing we only emphasize the fact that there is no way of interfering with the development of our sex life, and that we are pushed toward other people by a force that is quite outside our control. The word *Befriedigung*, on the contrary, applies in particular to the end of the sexual process, i.e., to the achievement of peace with someone of the opposite sex. It also implies that this moment of joy and reconciliation was preceded by all sorts of hostilities, and that these were gradually overcome and left behind. Finally, it tells all those utopians dreaming of spiritual and bodily peace achieved once and for all that what we are talking about is only a process of pacification in a limited sphere. This process is never completed and only occurs in special moments of grace, which should never be taken as unfailing guarantees for the future. This is the point I shall discuss in the next and last chapter.

VIII

SEXUAL BOND AND PSYCHOLOGICAL BOND

We should devote our attention once again to the meaning of the word "bond." I have put it in the title, although I realize that it is very ambiguous. In the light of the process of psychological development that I have described, it is easy to see that it has different meanings at different levels. As a result of the dramatizations that take place in our fantasy lives, which I described in the chapter on internal conflicts (Chapter III), the term "sexual bond" carries with it in the early stages the connotation of the loss of freedom of movement. Two people who come together in a union do indeed seem at first to be abandoning their rights, each becoming the slave of the other or at least fearing this may occur. The popular expression to "get hitched" implies precisely a yoke around the neck. A number of myths and legends about bonds reflect this level of meaning. There are gods who are either bound or bind others; there is

"Prometheus Bound"; there is talk of the power of bonds, and so forth. This is surely a relic of the ancient fear of slavery. And it is just this fear, with its swarm of frightening symbols, that keeps a number of people away from a long-term or recognized union, because they have invented for themselves a picture of freedom which they are afraid of losing. What they are afraid of is being tied up for good, as if there were no difference between being a slave and being a partner in a sexual union. It is of course perfectly true that even successful intercourse is not always enough to bring about a psychological union between two partners. This does not mean that there is no desire for such a union, but that it is impaired by the terrifying image of slavery, supported by the no less frightening image of a dangerous, domineering personality who only surrenders in order to ensure a more effective grip in the long run. These images bring us to the heart of what I have called the inner conflicts, and reveal a sex life in which fear and hostility on both sides still play a large part.

At a higher level, the bond represents the declared intention of one partner to be faithful to the other for better or for worse, regardless of any temporary glances elsewhere. The engagement and wedding rings are symbols at this level. Here the bond is really and truly one of the great meaningful metaphors human beings have used since time immemorial for promising aid and mutual assistance, and for offering pledges for the future. Marriage rituals are full of this significant imagery, which, it is true, represents people's intentions rather than anything that they are psychologically able to achieve. All love affairs pass through the phases of gifts and oaths, and they will not be abolished by a handful of anarchical theorists. For it is in the nature of human anxiety that, sooner or later, we should ask anyone who gives us pleasure, joy or promise, for an oath of constancy. And it seems to me unreasonable to re-

ject commitments of this sort as being necessarily hypocritical. To do so would be to remove from the adventure
of love one of the most precious elements and one that is
required by its very nature. For it would deprive human
beings of a consecration, the need of which they probably
feel as much as they feel the need for physical love. In any
event, people do try to overcome the permanent tension
between the sexes, and one of their most valuable allies in
putting aside this hostility is the oath. Admittedly it requires long psychological preparation and is by no means
an end in itself. While it provides a solemn entry into life
in common, it is certainly not an infallible guarantee of
success. It is not a piece of magic that will automatically
turn married life into what those who commit themselves
to it hope it will be. The anarchists are right to reject both
marriage vows that are expected to have infallible results,
and oaths which people trust implicitly to ensure the success of their marriage and their love. I for one would agree
that there is nothing more abject than the husband or wife
who maintains that the vows made on one solemn day in
their lives give them the everlasting right of possession over
their partner's body. The fact that we have obtained these
solemn oaths does not mean that we can now abandon our
previous courteous behavior. Nor does our triumph in having finally captured the object of our desires release us
from continued efforts to bring our aggressions under control. Indeed, it may be unwise to point to the sacred nature
of the marriage vows and the obligations of wedlock as a
means of preventing either of the partners from having
sexual relations on the side. For we should never make an
improper use of sacred things; and certainly we should
never try to use them as the basis for mythical obligations.
The only result is inevitably to arouse hostility or mistrust.
While it may sometimes be expedient to remind married
couples of the more solemn moments of their love, this

should be done in a spirit of goodwill for the purpose of encouraging them to renew their pledges and of reminding them that in their own past there were declarations of affection that were probably as valid, if not more so, than their present conflicts. In any event, to insist exclusively on the obligatory nature of these vows (and therein lies the symbol of bondage) is really no more than a trick. For the individuals concerned can always reply that they did not understand the full significance of their mutual commitment, and that they were caught in a snare. On the contrary, to recall that at some time in their joint past they were sufficiently trusting and devoted to one another to swear eternal fidelity, and that they did so despite many doubts about the ways in which their desires and feelings might develop, will surely help remind them of their better selves. This is something quite different from using a sacred act as a form of constraint. In other words, the solemn declaration of love and fidelity must be only the first of a whole series of solemn acts and vows that will continue throughout the couple's life together. This solemn aspect of life in common should be renewed not only at anniversaries and birthdays, but also, for example, at the end of a period of disagreement between the partners. Nor do I mean by this that couples who despair and are unable at any given moment to surmount their tensions and renew their vows should be considered outcasts. But I am writing for the many people who wish to turn the sacred aspect of their union into a genuine psychological bond and to make a reality of the solemn fiction of the marriage ceremony.

This brings us to the last meaning of the words "bond," or "link." In addition to the fantasy image and the meaningful symbol, the word can refer to real behavior and real feelings. We say of two people that they are closely linked when their conduct harmonizes without too much difficulty, so that in the end one cannot do without the other. As in their sex lives, so the daily life of one depends on the daily life of the other. In practice this link takes the form of many small details: each puts up with the annoyances of necessary gainful work or household chores for the sake of the other, and moments of idleness are also periods of great intimacy. There are still conflicts, but they subside rather quickly and serve only to confirm from time to time that the underlying union is stronger than any temporary estrangement. Experience with life's difficulties brings with it a growing feeling of stability and even permanence. This psychological bond is still very frail when solemn vows are exchanged or when sexual relations finally take place. Indeed, it only matures after a very long period of living together, and can be said to be quite firm only after many years of trial and error. Many young people make the mistake of believing that it is already formed for life when they declare their love for each other. And it would surely be hypocritical to enter into this solemn bond pretending that no effort is needed to turn it into a psychological one; to do so would indeed be to act in the way so frequently condemned by contemporary writers and philosophers, those sworn enemies of what they like to call hypocrisy.

In the attempts to create a psychological bond, sexual relations raise a special problem. In accordance with laws that are now generally understood, animals and human beings alike generally become closely attached to things that give them satisfaction. And we know that sexual enjoyment is one of the greatest pleasures that anyone can have. It would therefore be reasonable to hope that if sexual intercourse were enjoyed a great many times with the same person, this would help to strengthen the bond. Unfortunately, in practice, it is clear that this is not so. For many couples, at any rate, repeated sexual intercourse obviously has no beneficial effect. Far from strengthening the psychological bond, it seems to relax and weaken it. It ought to be possible to find some explanation of this dramatic exception to the general rule that pleasure grows with the repetition of agreeable actions.

As this book is strictly limited to dealing with sexual behavior in normal human adults, I have deliberately made no reference to the pathological cases in which, owing to inhibitions arising from their unconscious, one of the partners, or both, never enjoy complete satisfaction. When this happens, hostility soon arises between them for very obvious reasons. At every attempt the partner is experienced either as a reminder of or as the cause of the individual's failure; it is quite natural to end up hating him or her, or looking for a more expert substitute. Many cases of infidelity arise from impotence or frigidity, and these are really no more than a search for some more exciting stimulant, which, it is hoped, will remove the "hang-up." But the temptation to look for sexual experience outside the marriage is also felt by normal couples, at least so far as momentary physical satisfaction is concerned. What goes on between the partners in a normal marriage to make such temptation dangerous, and what causes the years of living together to disunite them gradually without any serious clash, until suddenly there is a split that turns almost instantly into an unbridgeable chasm?

There is one common answer: the drift apart is the result of habit. But, if I may say so once again, the habit of great pleasure enjoyed in common should surely strengthen the bond between the partners. It would be more accurate to lay the responsibility at the door of habit, arising from acts that may remain physically the same but which come to have less and less meaning. And for a certain number of unfortunate couples sexual relations do seem to become automatic. All the dramatic, expressive and meaningful aspects disappear or are neglected by a sort of laziness that arises from the feeling of one partner that he or she has rights over the other. This type of laxity, in the end, makes the sex act as regular and physiological as eating, and it does so to the great detriment of self-expression, play, seduction and self-affirmation, the need for which is part of every human being's makeup.

I have shown that the progression from erotic stimulation to the consummation of intercourse with a partner of the opposite sex represents a long process of evolution, both internal and external, and that the main stages are the appearance of aggression, personal agitation and self-doubt, expression of contradictory tendencies, narcissistic seduction, submission and devotion to the loved one, and rites leading to the disappearance of suspicion on both sides. One reason I have deliberately refused to say that any of these stages takes place in a given age bracket is that none of them is ever left behind forever, and each recurs, though usually in a much accelerated form, every time sexual relations are renewed. Naturally, adolescence and youth are the times when narcissistic expression and development are most likely to take place. Similarly, in middle and old age couples have more placid feelings and the partners can enjoy each other's presence without much talk, remembering both the difficult times and the happy experiences that they have had together. But while certain basic patterns of behavior may change with age, the dialectic of human sex life is a built-in one and lasts as long as sex life itself. If the sex act is to be something more than a prescription for physical relief to be taken from time to time, and more like a genuine act of peace in the real sense of the word, it must be consummated as part of a life in which expression, seduction and devotion each has its proper place.

The habit of explaining things genetically in the modern scientific world tends to make us forget that behavior is largely dynamic and changing, and this is especially true in psychology. Sex life is not merely a collection or a series of sex acts. Far more importantly, it is part of a whole life, including man's fantasies, imagination, conquests, games and repeated triumphs over the elements of discord. After a few years together many couples still have sexual intercourse, but they no longer have any sex *life* with each other. They no longer play the childish games which allowed them to express unconscious conflicts, nor do they try to seduce one another. They would be embarrassed if they tried to repeat their declarations of love. In short, they have forgotten the great secret of being in love.

Naturally, all the stages I have described do not have to be gone through before each act of intercourse. I hope that readers will not accuse me of having any such crazy notion. The strength, rhythm, and length of each stage must change with the circumstances and with the partners' knowledge of one another. Things that took months before emotional relations were properly established may take only a few seconds—the duration of a word or a gesture—between partners who know each other well. But only if they remain sensitive to their partner's emotions and feelings will both of them find complete satisfaction in their intercourse.

Nor should we forget that every adult's sexuality remains exposed to every erotic stimulation coming from elsewhere. No love is ever strong enough to be completely final and immunize the partners against all new excitements. Despite every vow and every satisfaction enjoyed with a partner, the human body remains permanently accessible to stimulation from other people. Any couple that wishes to remain permanently together should be warned that there is no bond on earth that will prevent them from feeling the disturbing influences that surround them. There is only one way of preventing exposure to these outside influences from degenerating into libertinage or instability, and that is to endow the relationship between the two partners with all the intensity of feeling that human beings experience in their contact with the outer world. Perhaps one reason great artists often consider marriage far less satisfactory than unmarried relationships is that humanity has not so far seriously considered the possibility of endowing marriage with the richness of artistic and emotional life. And yet, it is only on these terms that marriage will not be a straitjacket. If two individuals are unable to play over and over again the games leading to tension and release, the bond that started to unite them will wither away. And then the influence of the outside world will be a permanent temptation; some will cease to struggle against it in the long run, while others will resist by becoming first repressed and then unable to accept their partner.

If, on the contrary, the relations between partners remain alive, and a flow of emotions and feelings of all sorts is maintained between them, their sex acts will bring them intense pleasure, not only in their bodies, which will be performing one of their most important functions, but also in their spirits, which will find complete release and the peace of fulfillment. The partners do not need to experience very many successful sex acts in the course of a week or a month for the psychological bond to be formed and strengthened. If one act of intercourse is especially satisfying after a rather monotonous period, that is all that is required to bring the two partners more lastingly together, and to make them not insensitive to outside influences, but able to resist their attractions.

Frequent consummation of the sex act between partners who are used to one another will not get rid of all the problems of daily life together, and success in the sex act is certainly not the be-all and end-all of human ambition. Only someone obsessed with sex would consider it as an end in itself, and those who consider the sex act and success in love, which is its epitome, as accomplishments in themselves, are blowing them up into something far more than they really are. There is of course no denying that successful intercourse brings with it moments of delightful peace, nor that it is a physical expression of the restoration of peace between two people previously kept apart by their own personalities and by hostility rooted in the misunderstandings that are part of daily life. But the awakening is always hard. After the visions and the moment of ecstasy, the partners have to return to their daily round, their roles in society, their own personalities and their separateness. This is the critical moment which pessimists use to throw discredit on the pleasure that has gone before. That everyone should return to their own lives is inevitable, and it is at these moments of comparative separation that erotic stimulations from outside have particular force. There is no point in talking of tendencies to polygamy or polyandry, of perverted Don Juanism or of the infinite nature of desire in order to describe the unsatisfied feeling that takes hold of everyone at the end of even the most successful sexual relations. Human beings are never fully developed, nor is their growth ever really complete. Whether alone or with others, they are never entirely shut off from outside influences, so that once normal existence reasserts itself, they are once again open to new stimuli. This is especially so because the sex urges of human beings are not only a matter of satisfying the hormones. The periodic release of tension will not prevent them from being sensitive to erotic shapes and movements. Imagination can produce new desires without any outside assistance even after successful intercourse. Men and women are endowed with memory and anticipation, both of which make them more permanently sensive to erotic stimuli than animals, and less sensitive to the fluctuations of their hormones. This leads me to

conclude that, knowingly or unknowingly, all human beings are stimulated at least to some degree by the sight of
anyone who has any sexual attractiveness. And it is, of
course, just in those parts of their existence which they
live separately from one another that men and women receive these numerous stimuli from outside. Moreover, the
feelings of sexual desire are likely to increase with each
new stimulus.

So, what is the difference between the flighty person who
gives in to each of these temptations and goes through all
the scenes of the drama of love with any passingly attractive individual, and the person who remains faithful to a
loved one? Is the former freer and less hypocritical than
the latter? Is there simply a difference in the depth of the
emotions or feelings? Is faithfulness simply a question of
repression, or the result of a voluntary refusal? There is no
doubt that very many different factors enter into the two
forms of behavior, and it is the job of modern psychology
to sort them out. First of all, even though there is still a
great deal that we do not know about these matters, clinical
observation seems to show that the difference between a
Don Juan and a faithful person is far less than those who
can overcome their attraction to the opposite sex only by
repression and denial would like to think. Second, it seems
that it is wrong to attribute such differences as do exist exclusively to conscious or voluntary factors.

In any event, faithful individuals do not differ from Don
Juans by being less sensitive to the many stimuli to which
they are open, and which come from all sides, since mankind abounds in seductive individuals. They certainly do
not feel the attractions of the people whom they meet any
less strongly than the Don Juans do, and they are just as
susceptible to the whole chain reaction which is by nature
quite blind—not attached to one person rather than another—but which tends to lead naturally to the consumma-

tion of the sex act. And it seems to me that this is where
the difference lies. Don Juan is impatient, and so does not
succeed in detaching all his feelings from anyone who has
momentarily succeeded in stimulating them. The faithful
individual keeps his feelings in reserve and prevents them
from concentrating on someone met in a chance encounter.
His emotional reserves, which at the level of primary feeling are no doubt rooted in a vague impersonal experience
of all the seductions in the world, are kept for the person
of his own choosing, with whom he has at least from time
to time succeeded in enjoying short periods of great physical and mental peace.

One reason faithful individuals are able to keep their
emotions in reserve in this way is the knowledge of all they
have already received from life with their spouse, and the
anticipation of what is still to come; and this applies not
only to sex life but also to the general tenor of life as a
whole. At this point I am not, as might be thought, defending a thesis based on utility, but simply stating things as I
see them. At first sight, a partner in a well-established
union may simply seem to be making a comparison between what he has, and is likely to go on having, in the satisfactions of his quiet life with his companion, and the
passing and uncertain pleasures to be obtained from an affair outside his regular union. But over and above this
type of calculation, at which the partner would certainly
be entitled to be vexed, there is something like the implicit
knowledge of the exceptional worth of a successful sex life.
While we should not try to pretend that people are nobler
than they are, we should equally not make the mistake of
thinking them less intelligent than they are. The achievement of bodily peace with an attractive partner is an experience which the beneficiaries are the first to extol, quite
apart from any principles involved; and they certainly wish
to ensure that there will be repetitions in the future, even

if this means foregoing certain other pleasures. Why should anyone who achieves sexual satisfaction be upset at seeing their partner looking for pleasure elsewhere unless they see this as a warning that something far more fundamental —their mental and physical harmony— is at stake? In most cases, when life is running fairly smoothly, partners who are able to overcome their separateness in successful intercourse at reasonable intervals form a sufficiently stable couple to be able to resist external attractions. If one of the partners continues to feel their pull, this means that the union is incomplete and that there is some failure in the partnership leading to a vague general feeling of discontent.

Of course, many shades and degrees of conduct are covered by the general term "fidelity." Some couples remain united because neither partner has strong sex feelings. Others remain constant because they feel that the moral obligation is more important than any physical harmony. Still others keep up appearances both for others and for themselves, but their imagination keeps wandering just the same. Then there are those who rightly wish to keep the family unit together because they consider it vital for the sake of the children they have created by their sexual activities; for this purpose they are prepared to forego new physical satisfaction even if they are no longer attracted to one another. The motives for constancy are thus legion, and they range from the basest to the noblest. But now that I have reached the end of this long analysis of the development of sex life in individuals, I wish to stress that there are partners whose physical and mental satisfaction is such that they do not need any adventitious motive for remaining constant. Despite the minor conflicts of daily life together, their experience of their bodily and emotional union, which admittedly varies from day to day and is sometimes more and sometimes less complete, is on the whole so satisfying that the sexual bond becomes a psychological one and they begin to fear any mishap that may upset it.

Should we go further and assume that in the most successful cases, the couple attain through their love a sense of universality, so that any sexual relations they might have with another partner could be seen only in the light of the satisfactions of their relationship with one another? The things that people have told me in confidence make me believe that there are men who have reached the point where even the most beautiful women seem to be only a less perfect manifestation of the woman they love, and that there are women who are reminded only of their own partner by seeing even the most attractive men. Neither the men nor the women I am talking about are unduly idealistic about their partners, but it is as if they have experienced such a degree of physical and mental union that any outside love affairs that might be put in their path by the chances of daily life seem to them to be only remote possibilities that would inevitably be less perfect than their actual state. Between Don Juan and the Constant Heart there is probably the same difference as between the idealist seeking absolute but unattainable Beauty through a large number of transitory forms, and the realist who finds universality in the deepening of a single special experience. Don Juan was seeking an ideal but nonexistent woman in every one whom he held in his arms. But the man I have described has done better than this, for he has succeeded with one particular woman in forming a relationship that is as intimate and special as anything possible to imagine within the limitations of mankind, and he has in addition found the quintessence of womanhood without looking for it. Similarly, it seems likely that it is not the promiscuous woman but the one who fulfills her sex life with a single man who enters most closely into the world of manhood as such.

I have slid away from psychological analysis into a discussion of the ideals or the standards that seem to appeal to mankind as a whole. But before I come to a close, I wish to counter one final objection, which is that I have omitted all mention of procreation, although that biological phenomenon is the most elementary and most obviously significant aspect of sexuality. I have done so deliberately because I wished to stay strictly in my field of psychological analysis. I would, however, add that a desire for children is not only part and parcel of our whole physical system, but it often also plays a part in the development of people's feelings toward one another. But my intention was to keep away from the moral questions raised by respect for human life, that is, more correctly, to show that in the process leading men and women to consummate the sex act with one another and to build up a lasting psychological bond, there is implicit a development toward a higher degree of humanity and hence a sort of fundamental morality, preceding and underlying what is normally meant by sexual morality. However, taking the facts just as they are, the establishment of a true and lasting sexual union would seem in itself to represent a victory over the powers of hate and perversion.

And this victory is not merely a matter of will or effort of mind; it also requires emotional maturity. This means that sexual behavior is something that develops over a period of time, and that its greatest successes are to be seen neither in the passing satisfaction of fickle desires nor in love that is obsessive and unyielding, but in the mutual surrender of two bodies imbued with ever-increasing affection and goodwill toward each other. This goodwill is its own reward, but if the union is blessed with children it will also be the best foundation for educating those children in the years to come.

INDEX